Praise for
Faithful Defian

"We best understand our times and ourselves by looking to history and to giants of the faith. We learn how they navigated their troubled times, modeling how to serve faithfully. We learn from their victories and their mistakes. This volume is a shining example of high-impact historical analysis and biography informing our current divisive times. Be inspired by Marshall Keeble's life and faith. Be challenged. Consider how to apply the lessons of this fascinating volume in your own life. You will be thrilled you did."

—**Michael O. Emerson,** Chavanne Fellow in Religion and Public Policy, Baker Institute for Public Policy at Rice University, and coauthor of *The Religion of Whiteness*

"In this engaging and impactful book, Leonard Allen sets the historical context for fresh perspectives on Marshall Keeble as a powerful evangelist, prolific church planter, and dedicated educator."

—**John Allen Chalk,** Whitaker Chalk Swindle & Schwartz; *Herald of Truth* radio speaker (1966–71)

"Keeble left an indelible mark on Churches of Christ. He presented as a docile, meek, almost subservient preacher before White philanthropists. But he was indefatigable in his pursuit of the building of the Lord's church and the saving of souls. While his pragmatism enabled him to endure unspeakable insults and abuse, his 'fruit' has sprung forth to challenge racial injustices in and out of the Churches of Christ."

—**Tanya Smith Brice,** editor of *Reconciliation Reconsidered: Advancing the National Conversation on Race in Churches of Christ*

"The common image of Marshall Keeble is worthy of a scholarly deconstruction. Thanks to the contributions in this volume, we gain a deeper understanding of the complexity of Keeble's work, ideology, and practice. It will please some and likely displease some; either way it draws us into the crucible of race for these times."

—**Lawrence W. Rodgers,** author of *Inward Revolution: A Journey of Radical Transformation*

"What an encompassing and engulfing look into the legacy of an historical figure whose influence continues to shape our brotherhood today! Walking through Marshall Keeble's life using various contextual lenses is insightful, inspirational, and impactful."

—**Jonathan Morrison,** minister, Cedar Crest Church of Christ, Dallas, Texas

FAITHFUL DEFIANCE

FAITHFUL DEFIANCE

Marshall Keeble's Life and Legacy

C. LEONARD ALLEN

EDITOR

Abilene Christian University Press

FAITHFUL DEFIANCE

Marshall Keeble's Life and Legacy

ACU PRESS

ISBN 978-1-68426-214-4 | LCCN 2024034681

Printed in the United States of America

LIBRARY OF CONGRESS CATALOGING-IN-PUBLICATION DATA
Names: Allen, Leonard, 1952- editor.
Title: Faithful defiance : Marshall Keeble's life and legacy / C. Leonard Allen, editor.
Description: Abilene, Texas : Abilene Christian University Press, [2025] |
Includes bibliographical references.
Identifiers: LCCN 2024034681 (print) | LCCN 2024034682 (ebook) | ISBN 9781684262144 (paperback) |
ISBN 9781684268443 (ebook)
Subjects: LCSH: Keeble, Marshall, 1878-1968.
Classification: LCC BX7077.Z8 K45 2025 (print) | LCC BX7077.Z8 (ebook) |
DDC 286.6/34092 [B—dc23/eng/20241026
LC record available at https://lccn.loc.gov/2024034681
LC ebook record available at https://lccn.loc.gov/2024034682

Cover design by Bruce Gore
Interior text design by Sandy Armstrong, Strong Design

Cover photo: Marshall Keeble baptizing, Bradenton, Florida, 1931

For information contact:
Abilene Christian University Press
ACU Box 29138
Abilene, Texas 79699

1-877-816-4455
www.acupressbooks.com

25 26 27 28 29 30 31 // 7 6 5 4 3 2 1

Dedicated to David Thomas,
September 15, 1935–April 11, 2024

Churchman, missionary, teacher, and administrator, Dr. Thomas served Freed-Hardeman University from 1959–2000. He established the Carroll B. Ellis Symposium at Lipscomb University, which sponsored the seminar that served as the basis for this volume.

"Keeble's humility was genuine, but was founded on the bravado of Brer Rabbit, who in countless slave tales outwits the Fox and the Bear by pitting his weakness against their strength. No one in his time and place possessed more formidable psychological and rhetorical weapons than Keeble or wielded them more effectively."

—Don Haymes

CONTENTS

PART 3
Marshall Keeble: His Legacy

ACKNOWLEDGMENTS

This volume was born through the Carroll B. Ellis Symposium at Lipscomb University in September 2023. We were honored to have Fred D. Gray, noted Civil Rights attorney and one of Marshall Keeble's "preacher boys," as one of the speakers on that occasion. He told of his years at Nashville Christian Institute as a young teenager and recounted his memorable fundraising trips with Keeble. At a reception that day, a portrait of Dr. Gray, commissioned by "Friends of Fred Gray" and painted by the renowned portrait artist Michael Shane Neal, was unveiled. (In June 2024 it was announced that the portrait had been acquired by The Smithsonian's National Portrait Gallery for its permanent collection.)

Scott Sager's partnership in the planning and conduct of the symposium was crucial to its success. And Candice McQueen, president of the university, encouraged and supported this event all along the way. The program included a panel of ministers, and we thank Robert Gardenhire (Schrader Lane Church of Christ, Nashville), Christopher Jackson (Jackson Street Church of Christ,

Nashville), and Anthony Walker (Highway 36 Church of Christ, Murphreesboro) for their participation.

A special acknowledgement is due to Marty and Jane Kittrell for a generous grant that made possible the publication and promotion of this volume.

I'm grateful for the research assistance of Mary Emily Bouldin and Sara Harwell at the Robert Hooper Archives, Beamon Library, Lipscomb University, and McGarvey Ice, director of Special Collections and Archives in the Center for Restoration Studies in the Brown Library at Abilene Christian University. And I owe a word of gratitude to John Mark Hicks, a contributor to this volume, for his research and editorial assistance.

C. Leonard Allen

Marshall Keeble, 1878–1968

INTRODUCTION

C. Leonard Allen

By 1960, Marshall Keeble (d. 1968) had been for decades the most well-known and effective evangelist in Churches of Christ. His gospel meetings often drew thousands of people, both Black and White, and he was in constant demand all across the South and beyond. Under his preaching, as many as forty thousand were baptized and an estimated three hundred congregations established.

This book takes a fresh and in-depth look at his life and legacy. He died in 1968, nearly sixty years ago. Such a distance provides us perhaps a clearer angle of vision from which to understand his life in his times. In this examination, we do not seek simply to praise and extol him—although there is much to extol. And we are not seeking simply to critique—although there are things to critique. We are seeking to better understand and appreciate the amazing fruit of his life—what Churches of Christ have received from him and from the heritage of faith that shaped him so profoundly.

Keeble in Context

The study of Christian history is a discipline that helps us see the nature of our faith heritage more clearly—its ideals and aspirations, the times that shaped it, the challenges it faced, the struggles it endured, the choices that key leaders made and how those choices played out. In the case of Marshall Keeble, the time that profoundly shaped him was a time of deep racial divide. It was also a time when the Stone–Campbell Movement had recently undergone a deep fracture, and Churches of Christ were forging their own separate identity apart from the Disciples of Christ. Doctrinal controversies abounded. Racial tensions abounded. What was "sound doctrine"? And who got to decide? The formative and constant controversies were conducted, as one historian well put it, as a "wild democracy."[1] It was a time when the identity of Churches of Christ was being re-formed and solidified, a time when churches—racially segregated churches—were being planted all over the South and well beyond. Marshall Keeble became a strong, effective, steadfast, colorful, and inspiring voice throughout those decades.

A small body of work on Keeble has emerged since his death. An early study was Arthur L. Smith Jr., "A Rhetorical Analysis of the Speaking of Marshall Keeble" (MA thesis, Pepperdine University, 1966). A doctoral dissertation by Forrest Neil Rhoads was titled "A Study of the Sources of Marshall Keeble's Effectiveness as a Preacher" (Southern Illinois University, 1970). The first biography was a short laudatory volume by J. E. Choate, *Roll Jordan Roll: A Biography of Marshall Keeble* (1974). A scholarly article appeared in 1977: Paul D. Phillips, "The Interracial Impact of Marshall Keeble, 1878–1968," *Tennessee Historical Quarterly* 36 (Spring 1977): 62–74.

The major—and groundbreaking—work on Keeble is Edward J. Robinson's *Show Us How You Do It: Marshall Keeble and the Rise of Black Churches of Christ in the United States, 1914–1968*, 2nd ed. (2008; University of Alabama Press, 2010); it remains the starting place for engaging Keeble's life and career. Robinson also prepared a companion volume, *A Godsend to His People: The Essential Writings and Speeches of Marshall Keeble* (University of Tennessee Press, 2008), making Keeble's writings readily accessible. Keeble also figures prominently in Robinson's recent book, *Hard-Fighting Soldiers: A History of African American Churches of Christ* (University of Tennessee Press, 2019). As our cultural context continues to change, we will continue to reassess and to gain new insights from the career of Marshall Keeble.

The Crucible of Race

Keeble's whole evangelistic career was spent in the context of strict segregation. An event from 1960 provides a glimpse into his everyday world. Keeble's traveling companion for ten years in the later part of his life was a much younger White preacher named Willie Cato. Their standard practice was for Cato to drive until well after dark, when they would stop at a motel for the night. Since Blacks were not allowed to stay in motels, Cato would park away from the main entrance, leave Keeble in the car, go into the motel lobby to secure a room, and then, under cover of darkness, slip Keeble into the room unnoticed. It usually worked. But during one night in Texas, they were awakened by a loud knocking on their door at about one o'clock in the morning; it was the manager telling them that Blacks were not allowed and that they must immediately vacate the room. They dressed quickly, got into their car, and drove into the night.[2]

This was the world of Marshall Keeble. The world of segregation was not only inconvenient and demeaning; it was dangerous and violent, especially for anyone who pushed back against it. Throughout the decade of the 1950s, as civil rights activism began to emerge, activists and their property increasingly became the objects of White violence. During this decade, more than 250

Black churches and homes in Alabama were firebombed, and the violence across the South continued into the 1960s, most famously in the 1963 bombing of 16th Street Baptist Church in Birmingham that killed four Black girls attending Sunday school and injured twenty-two others. In Mississippi alone during the 1964 Freedom Summer campaign, terrorists bombed twenty-nine homes and thirty-five Black churches. Numerous attacks took place in the states that border the Deep South as well, not just across the Deep South.[3] More widespread than the physical violence were various forms of political, economic, and social intimidation.

Marshall Keeble's fifty-five-year career as a full-time evangelist cannot be understood apart from this context.

Keeble's Times and Legacy

This book had its beginning with the Carroll B. Ellis Symposium on the campus of Lipscomb University in September 2023. Among the speakers that day was Fred D. Gray, one of Keeble's early "preacher boys," a lifelong preacher and elder in Churches of Christ and a distinguished civil rights attorney noted for his relentless efforts to break down segregation wherever he found it. His assigned topic that day was to share with us his relationship with Marshall Keeble. He told stories of himself as a thirteen-year-old boy accompanying Keeble on several multistate trips in the 1940s for the purpose of recruiting and fundraising for Nashville Christian Institute. And Gray spoke of his long friendship with Keeble over the decades and the deep respect they shared—even though Keeble did not share Gray's open commitment to the Civil Rights Movement. Gray's stories—and his tribute to Keeble—marked a high point of the day.

The first group of essays in this volume seeks to situate Marshall Keeble's life in the context of the late nineteenth and early twentieth centuries. Leonard Allen shows that when Keeble first emerged on the scene, Churches of Christ had just experienced division from the Disciples of Christ and were in the process of solidifying a separate identity. In that new identity, early themes of unity and restoration that had driven Alexander Campbell's movement had narrowed; restoration of the true gospel and true church, not unity, had become the primary focus. David Holmes situates Keeble in the context of the Black preacher in the United States, who in varied ways helped slaves cope with their oppression and, in the aftermath of slavery, helped Blacks endure the harsh burdens of segregation. And Edward Robinson lays out the seven factors that Keeble pointed to as explaining his evangelistic success; and he shows how seven men—four White and three Black—helped make Keeble the church planter that he became.

The second group of essays focuses on Keeble's preaching career. John Mark Hicks, drawing upon careful research in the early periodical sources, identifies four key areas in which Keeble followed the example of Samuel W. Womack, a deeply committed Black preacher (who also became Keeble's father-in-law). Edward Robinson points to the suffering and hard challenges that Keeble faced throughout his preaching life and then lays out Keeble's seven-point preaching strategy that guided him year after year. Robinson shows how Keeble became, in his later years, a moral counselor to younger preachers and an elder statesman for Black Churches of Christ, in addition to being an evangelist and church planter. Tanya Smith Brice focuses on the "Constant Challenge of Race," pointing to the various forms of racism, both more subtle and more blatant, that Keeble faced; and she shows that Keeble, although he never spoke out against segregation, believed in the concept of racial self-help, which impacted many of his preacher students.

The final group of essays focuses on Keeble's legacy. Jefferson Caruthers lifts up as Keeble's chief legacy a commitment to evangelism, to the training of effective preachers, and to Christian education; his successes in these areas—against strong odds—formed and empowered this legacy, which continues to stand as an inheritance to new generations. Edward Robinson, building on Fred Gray's notes from his Lipscomb symposium speech, shows how Keeble's influence shaped Gray as a young teenager at NCI and how that played out in later years: how Keeble's meek posture on race relations contrasted with Gray's bold public stance against racial discrimination and the White establishment. Orpheus Heyward focuses on another of Keeble's early "boy preachers": W. F. Washington, a powerful preacher who over the span of fifty years built one of the largest Black congregations in the United States, along the way becoming a defender of the faith as well as an open admirer of Martin Luther King Jr.

Finally, in a concluding essay, Leonard Allen shows that, following Keeble's death in 1968, many of the younger preachers influenced by him became open challengers of the racism that was endemic in American culture and among Churches of Christ; and that Black and White Churches of Christ during these years grew not closer but further apart, moving "from segregation to independence."[4] And now, lo these several decades later, we still find ourselves in a crucible of race. A crucible, we should remember, can be a place where one gets tested by fire and transformed in the refining process.

Nearly sixty years after Marshall Keeble's death, both Black and White churches face a new, increasingly post-Christian cultural landscape. Denominational labels are receding, and a new nondenominational spirit is rising. What might it mean in such a time to live out Churches of Christ's—and Keeble's—long-held claim to have risen above denominationalism?

NOTES

[1]David Edwin Harrell Jr., *Churches of Christ in the Twentieth Century: Homer Hailey's Personal Journey of Faith* (University of Alabama Press, 2000), 40.

[2]See Appendix One for the rest of this story, told by Cato's daughter Rita Cochrane.

[3]See the pamphlet "Intimidation, Reprisal and Violence in the South's Racial Crisis" (American Friends Service Committee, National Council of Churches, and the Southern Regional Council), https://dp.la/item/4a216084488e09638d8b936a7d4a66e0; the Mississippi statistics come from John Dittmer, *Local People: The Struggle for Civil Rights in Mississippi* (University of Chicago Press, 1994), 251.

[4]Wes Crawford, *Shattering the Illusion: How African American Churches of Christ Moved from Segregation to Independence* (Abilene Christian Univeristy Press, 2014).

PART ONE

MARSHALL KEEBLE

The Historical Times

CHAPTER ONE

THE RESTORATION MOVEMENT FROM CANE RIDGE TO MARSHALL KEEBLE

C. Leonard Allen

Marshall Keeble stood in the stream of the Restoration Movement associated with Barton Stone and Alexander Campbell in the early nineteenth century. But because his career emerged when the movement was over a hundred years old, he was shaped even more by the theology that Churches of Christ had hammered out in the late nineteenth and early twentieth centuries in their break with the Christian Churches / Disciples of Christ. By this time, the restoration theology had been through several permutations, and the founding vision had narrowed and hardened.

In this chapter, I want to locate Keeble in this robust and shifting tradition. All Christian traditions change from one generation to the next. Changes may be subtle, but the very process of passing on a set of beliefs inevitably alters them. So I am proposing that Marshall Keeble, in his basic theological commitments, was a product of what Churches of Christ had become by the early twentieth century.

Let me begin with three illustrations from Keeble's sermons and writings. One, of course, is his prominent use of the "five-finger exercise" developed by Walter Scott in the 1820s and based on Alexander Campbell's view of conversion. Keeble called it the "naked gospel," a gospel free of human dress or adornment. He used the image of a ladder reaching from the church down into the world. To become a member of the Lord's church, everyone must climb this five-rung ladder. The first rung is the command to hear the Word; the second rung is the need to believe it; the third is the call to repentance or reformation of life; the fourth is public confession of Christ; and the fifth rung is baptism in water for the remission of sins.[1] Most of his sermons focused on or at least included this five-step invitation.

Second is the rejection of all denominations and of their members as true Christians—a standard view he learned from David Lipscomb and his successors. "There is no authority in the word of God for any denominations," said Lipscomb. "All denominations are sinful; every one is formed by adding to the things God ordained." To form "a denomination is to form an institution of man over and above the churches or institutions of God." So if any people "obey the gospel among denominations, the voice of God is, 'Come out from among them'; and this they must do, if they expect to be saved."[2] Keeble embraced this view, calling fellow preachers "to fight the sectarians and the false doctrines they teach and call their names so they will know whom we are fighting."[3]

Third is a rational view of conversion that rejected all "spiritual operations" and the emotionalism often associated with it. Campbell had said many times that the true gospel bypasses all the emotional paraphernalia of revivalism, calling hearers simply to examine the biblical testimony, promptly believe it, and then "obey the gospel" (that is, be baptized). Conversion was a rational and orderly process. Keeble cast this key point in his own colorful and colloquial language: "The more of the word of God you got in you, the less emotionalism . . . the less excitement." He added that "when you accept the gospel of Jesus Christ, it knocks all the monkey notion out." Why is that? Because "the gospel is like lead, it's heavy, when you preach it to a man, it holds him down. He can't bounce around. . . . My friends, the bouncing time is over. It's time now to come down to real facts. Sit, study, drink down the truth."[4]

The Theological Context

Keeble's career emerged at a time when the Restoration Movement was a full century down the road from its modern beginnings. That beginning, to be precise, occurred with the Cane Ridge Revival of August 1801 and with Barton Stone's "Christian" movement that emerged in the aftermath of the revival. That is where the Southern Churches of Christ had their beginnings. Long before Alexander Campbell appeared on the scene with his rational gospel, these churches spread "like fire in dry stubble" through the backwoods of Kentucky, Tennessee, and northern Alabama, so that by 1810 or so there may have been as many as thirteen thousand members in several hundred mostly rural congregations.[5]

When Thomas and especially Alexander Campbell appeared on the scene in the 1820s, the Stone Movement was quickly (although not completely) transformed. The Stoneite Christians were especially attracted to the rational gospel of Campbell. In his reform movement, Campbell sought two basic things. As a counter to revivalism, he wanted a rational and orderly conversion process. Revivalism relied on a capricious and emotional process, and this kept people waiting—sometimes for months or years—on a conversion experience. And second, as a counter to denominationalism and its deep divisions, he sought a simple New Testament platform for unity. His movement was based on two foundational moves: a restoration of the "ancient gospel" and a restoration of the "ancient order of things." The "ancient gospel," far from a mysterious experience of the Spirit, was simply a process of believing simple facts, obeying a simple command, and then receiving spiritual blessings. The "ancient order" was the simple pattern of the church he thought was self-evident in the New Testament.[6]

These two restorations, Campbell believed, would open up a whole new era: Christians in the denominations would drop their denominationalism and come together in an unprecedented demonstration of unity. Campbell could exult that the "ancient gospel" would be "the instrument of converting the whole human race, and of uniting all Christians upon one and the same foundation." As this unity emerged, he believed, something even more wonderful would emerge: a millennial age—an unprecedented time of worldwide peace and prosperity—that would cover and bless the Earth. "Just insofar as the ancient order of things is restored," he declared in 1825, "just so far has the millennium commenced."[7]

The appeal of Campbell's message was strong, and the movement grew rapidly. In the 1820s and 1830s, Walter Scott—using the "five-finger exercise"—reported baptizing over a thousand people a year for many years. By about 1830, Campbell believed that the prospect for unity was bright—indeed, that it was virtually assured. If believers would "purify their speech" and "abandon every word and sentence not found in the Bible," nothing would be left but the "gospel facts" and division simply could not exist.[8] On January 1, 1832, Campbell's Disciples movement and Stone's "Christian" movement formally united, and the united movement continued to grow rapidly. For a while, it seemed unstoppable, as if Campbell's breathtaking vision for Christian unity was well on its way.

But this profound optimism soon began to recede, and with the coming of the Civil War, it collapsed. The vision of restoration as a means to unity split apart. Churches of Christ steadily coalesced around a strict patternist restoration of the first-century church, sidelining unity, while the Christian Churches / Disciples of Christ, by fits and starts, gradually coalesced around the unity impulse, sidelining restoration. The formal dating of the separation between Churches of Christ and Disciples of Christ in the 1906 US census came well after the deep breaking apart was mostly done.

During this first hundred years, the movement had undergone two momentous transformations. It had experienced an unlikely merger (in the early 1830s) and had undergone a deep fracture (in the late 1800s). And both of these transformations were accompanied by major theological adjustments.

Among those who became Churches of Christ, the original founding vision of the movement was refocused—narrowed, we could say. The twin themes of restoration and unity, which had characterized the first fifty years, were replaced by the predominant theme of restoration as an end in itself. The restoration of the true gospel and the true church became the primary focus, with the expectation for unity now a minor—or even forgotten—concern.

The separation of Churches of Christ from the Christian Churches before the turn of the century was followed by several decades of internal identity-forming controversy among Churches of Christ. In the words of one historian, the landscape became a "wild democracy," where various parties pressed their case for what comprised "the essentials."[9] There was, for example, sharp tension between the "Texas tradition"—leaders like Austin McGary, R. L. Whiteside, and Foy Wallace Jr.—and the "Nashville tradition," with James Harding, David Lipscomb, J. N. Armstrong, and others. Keeble embraced the Texas tradition on rebaptism—Baptists had to be rebaptized since they had been baptized improperly and thus were not Christians. On most other matters, Keeble went with the Nashville tradition and the *Gospel Advocate*. By the 1930s, something close to a doctrinal consensus was emerging among Churches of Christ; it was epitomized in five small volumes titled *Sound Doctrine* (1920–25) by C. R. Nichol and R. L. Whiteside. Keeble's theology was almost precisely in line with it.

The Social Context

If the new orthodoxy of Churches of Christ was the *theologial* context for Keeble's career, the legacy of slavery and strict Jim Crow segregation that arose out of it was the *social* context. Here too, let me trace the trajectory of the Restoration Movement.

Churches influenced by Barton Stone and the revival began to insist, decades before the Civil War, that one could not be a Christian and hold slaves. Stone recalled that shortly after the close of the Cane Ridge Revival, his "mind became unearthly, and was solely engaged in the work of the Lord. I had emancipated my slaves from a sense of right, choosing poverty with a good conscience, in preference to all the treasures of the world." Indeed, he noted, "This revival cut the bonds of many poor slaves."[10] This strong emancipationist impulse was rooted in a theology of God's kingdom coming. Stone believed that, in the power of the Spirit, God's kingdom was already breaking into the present and that a disciple's citizenship in that kingdom superseded all other commitments.[11] Throughout the rest of his life, Stone sought to live out this strong countercultural stance. Nearly thirty-five years after Cane Ridge (1835), Stone could declare, "I have long viewed Slavery as the darkest cloud that hangs over America."[12]

This theology of the kingdom was carried forward by David Lipscomb. In the decades following the war, Lipscomb insisted that local congregations—in sharp contrast to the churches under the sway of Jim Crow segregation—be integrated as an exhibition of the nature of God's kingdom, which breaks down all such hostile barriers. He insisted that baptism must trump all other allegiances—like "Union" or "Confederate," White or Black—and that for Christians to maintain the animosities and separations of the culture was a tragic violation of the meaning of one's baptism.

Yet, at the same time, Lipscomb could embrace the racial paternalism that was common among Christians in his time. From the 1860s through the 1880s, he expressed his belief that because Blacks—the "freedmen"—were unprepared for freedom, they would likely die out if not aided, like children, by White brothers and sisters. Underlying this paternalism was the belief that slavery had actually helped Blacks reach "the highest degree of intelligence and civilization reached by the African race for two thousand years."[13]

The Civil War had ended slavery but not the deep culture that slavery had produced over generations. In the South, the perceived inferiority of the Black race was deeply ingrained and provided the foundation for a new regime of strict segregation maintained by Jim Crow legislation. In the wake of Reconstruction, Whites of the ex-Confederate South constructed a powerful culture-defining separation of Blacks and Whites, maintaining White racial supremacy. Between 1890 and 1940, argues Grace Hale, "the [new] culture of segregation turned the entire South into a theater of racial difference, a minstrel show writ large upon the land."[14] It was held firmly in place by comprehensive Jim Crow legislation (and by violence), and it remained mostly in place until the 1960s.

Churches of Christ, which were still in the process of forming a new identity after the division with the Christian Church, generally embraced the racial separations with little resistance. Like the other Southern Christian traditions, they accommodated a deeply oppressive—and often violent—segregation. One key reason was the diminishment and virtual loss of the kingdom theology that had marked Barton Stone and his heirs like David Lipscomb. This theology had prioritized God's kingdom over all earthly kingdoms. It accepted that the primary allegiance to God's rule sometimes meant turning one's back on human laws and dominant cultural values—and paying a sharp price for one's nonconformity.[15]

David Lipscomb spoke out of this vision throughout the second half of the century. "The great weakness of the church today," he wrote in 1889, "is that the children of God enter into the kingdoms of this world, imbibe the spirit of those kingdoms, bring that spirit into the church of God, defile the church and drive out the spirit of Christ."[16] So he counseled Christians to maintain their primary allegiance to God's kingdom by refusing to get caught up in the kingdoms of this world—including not becoming combatants in the military, not accepting the cultural insistence on racial segregation, and even not voting.

Lipscomb thought that racial segregation was a glaring and ongoing sin among disciples of Jesus. "Nothing is more clearly taught in the Bible," he wrote in 1878, "than that Christ came into the world to break down middle walls, family prejudices, natural animosities, race antipathies, and to unite the different kindreds, tongues and tribes into one undivided and indivisible brotherhood."[17] Lipscomb maintained this position into the early twentieth century (he died in 1917). But his strong words went largely unheeded. Separate and segregated congregations became the norm everywhere, although Blacks and Whites could sometimes join together in evangelistic efforts—as we see in Marshall

Keeble's career. And regarding the strict requirements of segregation in Southern culture, silence and the status quo reigned.

Conclusion

Lipscomb's radical outlook on a world in rebellion against God characterized a strong minority among Churches of Christ in the latter nineteenth century. But in the early twentieth century, this theological outlook sharply receded. Some openly denounced Lipscomb's kingdom theology as heresy. Among most members, caught up in the patriotism of two world wars, it was simply ignored or forgotten.[18] And so it mostly remains today.

As this shift occurred in the early twentieth century, the theology of Churches of Christ became more rigid and doctrinaire, harder-edged and exclusive. Churches of Christ could now view themselves unabashedly and without hesitation as the one true church, as the kingdom of God restored to the earth. At the same time, the sense of separation from the world gradually declined. In the twentieth century, Churches of Christ steadily became more content with conventional moral standards (including the segregationist status quo), more taken with the American civil religion, and more concerned about respectability.[19]

This was the context in which Marshall Keeble became an evangelist and church planter. This was the context in which Keeble's strong gifts, steadfastness, toughness, and tactical navigation of the Black/White divide enabled him to baptize perhaps as many as forty thousand people, to plant over three hundred congregations throughout the South, and to raise up and mentor powerful sons and grandsons in the faith. Marshall Keeble, more than any other African American leader in Churches of Christ, propelled the astounding growth of Black Churches of Christ in the twentieth-century South.

NOTES

[1]*Biography and Sermons of Marshall Keeble, Evangelist* (Gospel Advocate, 1931), 57–61.

[2]David Lipscomb and E. G. Sewell, *Questions Answered* (Gospel Advocate, 1921). This was a compilation of answers to questions from readers of the *Gospel Advocate* over several decades.

[3]Marshall Keeble, "Among the Colored Brethren," *Gospel Advocate* 96 (Mar. 4, 1954): 83, cited by Edward J. Robinson, *Show Us How You Do It: Marshall Keeble and the Rise of Black Churches of Christ in the United States, 1914–1968* (University of Alabama Press, 2008), 60.

[4]*Biography and Sermons of Marshall Keeble*, 38.

[5]R. L. Roberts and J. W. Roberts, "Like Fire in Dry Stubble—The Stone Movement, 1804–1832 (Part I)," *Restoration Quarterly* 7 (1963): 148–58; Roberts and Roberts, "Like Fire in Dry Stubble—The Stone Movement (Part II)," *Restoration Quarterly* 9 (1965): 26–40.

[6]For a summary of this restoration agenda, see C. Leonard Allen, *Things Unseen: Churches of Christ in (and after) the Modern Age* (Leafwood, 2004), 45–53.

[7]Alexander Campbell, "A Restoration of the Ancient Order of Things, no. 1," *Christian Baptist* 2 (Feb. 7, 1825): 136.

[8]Alexander Campbell, "A Restoration of the Ancient Order of Things, no. 17. Purity of Speech," *Christian Baptist* 4 (Mar. 1826): 154.

[9]David Edwin Harrell Jr., *The Churches of Christ in the Twentieth Century: Homer Hailey's Personal Journey of Faith* (University of Alabama Press, 2000), 40, 44.

[10]Barton W. Stone, *The Biography of Eld. Barton Warren Stone, Written by Himself with Additions and Reflections by Eld. John Rogers* (J. S. and U. P. James, 1847), 44.

[11]See Richard T. Hughes, "'The Politics of the Day' and 'The Politics of Heaven': The Apocalyptic Orientation of Barton W. Stone," in *Resisting Babel: Allegiance to God and the Problem of Government*, ed. John Mark Hicks (Abilene Christian University Press, 2020), 15–35.

[12]Barton Stone comments preceding William Lloyd Garrison, "Address to the People of the United States on Slavery," *Christian Messenger* 9 (Apr. 1835): 82. See Newell Williams, "Pursuit of Justice: The Antislavery Pilgrimage of Barton W. Stone," *Encounter* 62 (Fourth Quarter, 2001).

[13]David Lipscomb, "Notes on Travel," *Gospel Advocate* 9 (July 25, 1867): 584, cited by Jefferson Caruthers, "Melting Away as Snow: David Lipscomb and the Freedmen, 1865–1880" (unpublished paper, 1989).

[14]Grace Elizabeth Hale, *Making Whiteness: The Culture of Segregation in the South, 1890–1940* (Random House, 1998), 284.

[15]Allen, *Things Unseen*, 35–38.

[16]David Lipscomb, *Civil Government: Its Origin, Mission, and Destiny, and the Christian's Relation to It* (Gospel Advocate, 1889).

[17]Lipscomb, "Race Prejudice," *Gospel Advocate* (Feb. 1878): 120–21.

[18]Allen, *Things Unseen*, 109–12.

[19]See Michael Casey, "From Pacifism to Patriotism: The Emergence of Civil Religion in the Churches of Christ During World War I," *Mennonite Quarterly Review* 66 (July 1992): 376–90.

CHAPTER TWO

THE RISE AND ROLE OF THE BLACK PREACHER IN AMERICA

David G. Holmes

My first experience as a preacher came when I was fifteen years old, some forty-six years ago. I have never preached full-time, nor have I ever been particularly skilled at the craft. But I am better for trying to be. Carroll Pitts Jr. was the main Black preacher who poured into my life. He was a protégé of R. N. Hogan, who was a student of pioneer preacher G. P. Bowser (1874–1950). Brother Pitts modeled for me the call to selflessly serve family, church, and community. As a teenager, I marveled at the oratorical excellence demonstrated by preachers who held gospel meetings in my home congregation or elsewhere in Los Angeles, including Dr. David Jones, Nashville, Tennessee; Dr. Jack Evans, Terrell, Texas; Dr. Roosevelt Wells, Harlem, New York; and Dr. W. F. Washington, Fort Lauderdale, Florida. As a teenage preacher, I knew that I would never attain their heights of rhetorical and biblical mastery, but they gave me something to aim for.

Marshall Keeble was a key shaper of this twentieth-century tradition of Black preachers among Churches of Christ. As the Stone–Campbell Movement fractured in the late nineteenth century and Churches of Christ began to form a separate identity in the opening years of the twentieth century, Keeble helped set the foundation for the new and eventually burgeoning stream of Black preachers. He himself had been powerfully influenced by the Black evangelist Samuel W. Womack (1851–1920) and went on to raise up a host of preaching "sons" and "grandsons" in the twentieth century.[1]

In this chapter, we want to set Womack and Keeble's lineage of Black preachers in Churches of Christ against the backdrop of the larger story of the Black church and its preachers in the United States.

From the American colonial period all the way down to the Civil Rights Movement, the Black church has served the economic, educational, social, and political needs of its members when mainstream society either refused to do so or did so poorly. The role of its preachers has necessarily been varied: sometimes prophetic, often conformist, and necessarily pastoral. The preaching styles have been characterized by passionate and interactive engagement with the congregation, and this distinctive feature of Black preaching—the "call and response," for example—was a means of addressing the long Black experience of abuse and suffering. The Black church also served as the space where many young people first nurtured their potential talents, skills, and competencies. Many who became well-known singers, actors, lawyers, and preachers first found their voice in the haven of segregated Black congregations.

Black Preachers as Prophets

Aside from the African American experience, religion has been routinely and widely used to critique oppression. Notable scholars like Sacvan Bercovitch have traced the Puritans' escape from Europe to America as a twofold biblical endeavor.[2] The journey itself was a type of exodus from European religious oppression. Prophetic critique of this oppression (the jeremiad) was the basis for the Puritans' exodus. Named for the prophet Jeremiah, the "jeremiad" depicts a form of theological critique directed at whatever powers may be oppressing. Enslaved and, later, segregated African Americans adapted the jeremiad to condemn the domination that they experienced within the United States. Many Black preachers would never be political enough to be labeled prophetic. Nevertheless, like the Minor Prophets, many Black preachers committed themselves to speaking truth to power. As I summarized in *Where the Sacred and Secular Harmonize*:

> African Americans also appealed to the jeremiad from exposing the sins of slavery and later segregation to envisioning, albeit ever so dimly, America's prospects of becoming the inclusive nation that God called it to be. However, the African American exodus was never confined to international geography. Their promised land was not to be found in another country as it had been for the Puritans. A wholesale spiritual conversion of white enslavers and later segregationists would contribute to full enfranchisement for black people and would transform America into the promised land.[3]

According to David Howard-Pitney, the rhetoric of the African American jeremiad would extend from David Walker through the Civil Rights Movement and into the 1990s.[4] Similarly, as African Americans extended the Exodus narrative from enslavement through segregation, they also dubbed a variety of their male and female leaders as Moses figures.

Black Preachers as Conformists

Beyond the prophetic office, Black preachers from the eighteenth through the nineteenth centuries represented a range of callings.[5] Some were called to preach for predominantly White congregations, North and South. Still others preached to their fellow enslaved on the plantation. Enslavers expected their Black preachers to teach their enslaved brethren to submit to all their master's will, wishes, and whims. And most of the Black preachers would comply at the plantation church while the master was watching. But several scholars tell us that many enslaved folks would slip away from the plantation to the brush arbors or woods for a different kind of worship.[6] There, the preacher would preach a more culturally authentic sermon—one rooted in love, justice, and hope. In his seminal 1972 work, *The Black Preacher in America*, Charles V. Hamilton summarized Black preachers' contrasting approaches to addressing slavery:

> Slavery was finally ended as a consequence of the Civil War. Throughout the nearly 250 years of its existence in this country, black preachers played roles that covered the spectrum: from the Reverend Jupiter Hammon who admonished slaves to look for happiness in the next world only; to those such as Reverend Richard Allen who condemned slavery but counseled slaves to love and obey their masters, because God would take care of the evil institution of human bondage; to those like Reverend Daniel Coker who advocated and personally pursued black colonization in Africa; to the Reverend Nat Turner who felt commanded by God to lead a violent revolt against slavery.[7]

Black preachers began participating in politics during Reconstruction following the period of American enslavement and the Civil

War. By the twentieth century, many Black preachers who had ascended to the national political stage began at the local level and built up a following. During the twentieth century, Black preachers' attitudes toward resistance ran the gamut from maintaining the social status quo to advocating self-defense against White racist violence to Martin Luther King Jr.'s nonviolent resistance. It is not surprising, therefore, that attitudes toward Black liberation and social justice within the Stone–Campbell preaching tradition would also vary widely. While Marshall Keeble might be considered a status quo accommodationist regarding Black rights, G. P. Bowser (1874–1950) possessed an activist mindset, as did most of the preachers who can be called Keeble's spiritual "grandsons."[8]

Black Preachers as Pastors

The story of the Black preacher in the United States is also the story of personal vocation. Black preachers served their congregations in many ways beyond the pulpit. On balance, the Black preacher was a jack of most trades, in addition to sharing the Word from the pulpit. He was also a counselor, adviser, mediator, and coach. For their congregants or flock, Black preachers were as likely to show up at the schoolhouse and courthouse as they were the church house. This is because Black preachers felt called to partner with their members through the trials and tribulations of nineteenth-century enslavement and twentieth-century Jim and Jane Crow segregation. African American preachers also exemplified practical wisdom, courage, and resilience. They modeled how Black America has creatively addressed religious, social, and political tensions. Whether or not African American preachers became politicians, they had to serve members of their congregation politically in the purest sense of that word.

Black Preachers and Their Flocks

The story of the Black American preacher is not only a story of American history and individual vocation. When Black preachers preach, they engage in a rhetorical enterprise—sometime deliberative, other times improvisational, but always imaginative and inspirational. For at the center of any story is how, why, and to whom you communicate. While there were and are Black congregations that worship in a more subdued fashion, the hallmark of Black churches has been fervent worship punctuated by the passionate exchange (known as "call and response") between preacher and congregation. The African American sermon was and is one of few formal speeches where the content can be reimagined or restructured by a real-time audience response.

To outsiders, the level of emotional exchange between some Black preachers and their congregations may seem over-the-top. Yet most scholars and practitioners of Black preaching would affirm that these expressions represent more than emotion for the sake of emotion. In his classic text, *Say Amen, Brother!*, William H. Pipes notes a connection between Aristotle's categories for effective persuasion (ethos, pathos, and logos) with Black folk preaching.[9] To oversimplify, for Aristotle, a public speaker establishes credibility through three appeals: ethos (ethical), logos (logical), and pathos (emotional). Pipes claims that in Black preaching, the emotional appeal is more prominent than the other two appeals.

Pipes's interpretation may represent a slight misreading of Aristotle's rhetoric in comparison to African American preaching. Aristotle was a philosopher trying to redeem the practice of public rhetoric from the widespread deception and manipulation that had characterized it for decades. Granted, history does record Black sophists who, like their White counterparts, have used preaching to manipulate the masses and milk them for their resources. But Black American preachers, for the most part, were ethical messengers of God to their people.

For African American preachers, this mostly ethical but also passionate and logical commitment to preaching was emphasized through three of the five classical canons of rhetoric: memory, style, and delivery. Preachers learned to memorize Scripture during the period of enslavement, when it was against the law for the enslaved to learn to read. For decades following enslavement, even when the pastors were not the most literate in all subjects, they were likely the most biblically literate. Reciting Scripture from memory became a tradition within Black churches. So vital and expected was the memorization of Scripture that Marshall Keeble's young preaching protégés, as they accompanied him on tours, would impress audiences with the reciting of long portions of Scripture. And it was not surprising that the legendary Church of Christ Black preacher R. N. Hogan was known as a "walking Bible." Still, *how* one recited Scripture (verbal flourish and animated gestures) became intertwined with *what* text was recited.

In short, Black preachers used intense passion to identify with their parishioners' cultural sensibilities as well as to help lift them out of the sense of hopelessness they experienced outside the walls of the church. Over the history of Black preaching, rarely have emotional displays been for their own sake. Rather, emotional expression within Black worship is at once uplifting and cathartic. The ebb and flow of singing, testifying, and shouting are timeless experiences tethered to a collective sense of *the back then*, *right now*, and *someday*. In this way, Black preaching is a part of the larger African American oral tradition. Rooted in West African cultural practices, the African American oral tradition infuses other expressive dimensions of Black culture. As Dolan Hubbard remarked, "The black oral tradition utilizes the structure that has become associated with improvisation and jazz but that we know more appropriately can be attributed to the sermon. This structure reflects the elasticity of African American culture and the African continuum."[10]

This is not to say that the context, style, and content of Black American preaching was monolithic. All Black preachers did not preach the same way. However, given how literacy was weaponized to denigrate the humanity of Blacks, cultural style and sermonic content had to be more closely integrated. Or, as James Henry Harris suggests, "Preaching style is not the antithesis of content but a corollary or constituent element of the content and hermeneutics (theory) of preaching. If the task of hermeneutics is to bridge the distance between text and interpreter (or listener), the orality and gestures of the preacher often contribute to the effectiveness of preaching."[11]

Black preaching has usually been demonstrative and animated precisely because Blacks were physically and psychologically abused. The fervent reading of and preaching from the text became indivisible. Both homiletics (the art of preaching) and hermeneutics (the science of interpretation) were and are matters of body, mind, and spirit.

This organic hermeneutic encompassing body, mind, and spirit was the only way Blacks could survive and, in many instances, thrive through the horrors of enslavement and segregation. This living hermeneutic also enabled Blacks to envision a sense of community among themselves, an affinity with White Americans, and an allegiance to the very nation that had oppressed them. At its loftiest, biblical interpretation is about more than making meaning from the text. It is about finding meaning in one's struggles through the text. Vincent L. Winbush has observed, "Rather than an end in itself, interpretation seemed actually to have been understood as the collective freed consciousness and imagination of African slaves (and the generations to follow) as they heard the biblical stories and retold them to reflect their own actual social situations, as well as reflect their visions for a different world order."[12] Freedom is the ultimate individual and collective aspiration. The Black preacher answered the unique calling of guiding folks to physical and spiritual freedom.

Bearing Witness as a Black Preacher

For me, the story of the Black American preacher is a personal story. My experience as a boy preacher expanded my passions beyond the pulpit. Preaching inspired me to take my education more seriously by sparking my curiosity for subjects outside of African American expressive culture. Before I wrote my first book, I learned to love the book of books through hearing great African American preachers. My perception of myself as a Christian scholar was born in the cradle of a South Central Los Angeles African American church. By the time I earned the rank of full professor in 2008, I had fully integrated my university teaching, professional presentations, research, and preaching into a holistic sense of vocation. In a few instances, one could scarcely discern where one practice ended and the other began.

Growing up in the Black church and being mentored by Black preachers has injected within me a piercing sense of personal accountability. There were other Los Angeles-based preachers, in addition to Carroll Pitts, who modeled for me the character to which I should aspire, not just as a Black preacher but as a Christian man. They include the late Dr. Calvin Bowers, the late John Green, the late Kinwood Devore, and Dr. Billy Curl. For every congregation for which I preach, for every student I teach, and for every person I reach, they matter.

I am not the best husband, father, or grandfather. But I am better than I might have been because I have known Black preachers who practiced what they preached. They refused to allow the worldly prejudices from the outside or the pastoral pressures from the inside to keep them from Paul's aspirational goal for all of those who have named the name of Christ: "If then you were raised with Christ, seek those things which are above" (Col. 3:1 NKJV). So, let the spirit of the African American preacher rise.

NOTES

[1]Edward J. Robinson, "'The Two Old Heroes': Samuel W. Womack, Alexander Campbell and the Origins of Black Churches of Christ in the United States," *Discipliana* 65, no. 1 (Spring 2005): 3–20.

[2]Sacvan Bercovitch, *The American Jeremiad: Studies in American Thought and Culture* (University of Wisconsin Press, 2012).

[3]David G. Holmes, *Where the Sacred and Secular Harmonize: Birmingham Mass Meeting Rhetoric and the Prophetic Legacy of the Civil Rights Movement* (Cascade, 2017), 10.

[4]David Howard-Pitney is considered one of the foremost scholars of the African American Jeremiad. David Howard-Pitney, *The African American Jeremiad: Appeals for Justice in America* (Temple University Press, 2005).

[5]This paragraph summarizes more comprehensive treatments of Black preaching history. See Henry H. Mitchell, *Black Preaching: The Recovery of a Powerful Art* (Abingdon Press, 1990), chapter 2.

[6]Also called "hush harbors," these covert religious meetings were among the few places where the enslaved could fully be themselves as Africans and Christians. They could freely share in sermon themes and African rituals that were off limits under the enslaver's supervision. See Mitchell, *Black Church Beginning: The Long-Hidden History of the First Years* (Eerdmans, 2004), 9–10, 13, 27, 33–34, 163.

[7]Charles V. Hamilton, *The Black Preacher in America* (William Morrow and Company, 1972), 68.

[8]On Bowser's racial outspokenness, see Crawford, *Shattering the Illusion*, 87–95; on Keeble's "grandsons," see Robinson, *Show Us How You Do It*, 155–72.

[9]William H. Pipes, *Say Amen, Brother! Old-Time Negro Preaching: A Study in American Frustration* (Wayne State University Press, 1992), 168, 190, 192.

[10]Dolan Hubbard, *The Sermon in the African American Literary Imagination* (University of Missouri Press, 1994), 7–8.

[11]James H. Harris, *The Word Made Plain: The Power and Promise of Preaching* (Fortress Press, 2004), 77.

[12]Vincent L. Winbush, *The Bible and African Americans: A Brief History* (Fortress Press, 2003), 28.

CHAPTER THREE

THE SHAPING OF A BLACK PREACHER

Edward J. Robinson

In 1965, Beverly Briley (1914–80), mayor of Nashville, Tennessee, honored Marshall Keeble's birthday (1878–1968) by giving him a bronze plaque. The inscription read, "In grateful recognition of Marshall Keeble for his long-time service to his God and to his fellowman, preaching and teaching the gospel, baptizing thirty thousand souls and establishing 350 congregations. His life's work including his appointment as President Emeritus of Nashville Christian Institute is a shining example of good citizenship."[1] Marshall Keeble left an indelible mark on the history of African American Churches of Christ. Yet he was not a self-made man. Many different people molded and shaped his life as a preacher.

Born in the decade of the 1870s, Marshall Keeble and his family felt the rumblings of racial turbulence sweeping across the South. Indeed, when congressional members asked Abraham Brumfield, a Black man in York County, South Carolina, about the Ku Klux Klan's raid in his community, he replied, "Well, they came to my house about midnight . . . some time in March. . . . When I saw death coming I got out."[2] What was true for Abraham Brumfield also held true for countless Black Southerners who found themselves subjected to racial violence years after the Civil War. In this hostile world emerged Marshall Keeble, who would later become the premier evangelist in African American Churches of Christ.

Seven Factors

When asked in the 1930s to account for his evangelistic success, Marshall Keeble, while preaching in Southern California, mentioned seven important factors. First, he said his wife, Minnie (Womack) Keeble (1880–1933), was at the "bottom of his preaching career." Second, his father-in-law, S. W. Womack (1851–1920), taught him the plan of salvation. Third, in around 1914, Keeble committed his life to full-time evangelism. Fourth, White leaders Samuel H. Hall (1877–1961), Nicholas B. Hardeman (1874–1965), and Filo B. Srygley (1859–1940) contributed significantly to his ministerial development. Fifth, Keeble understood the importance of "staying in place" in the South, where race relations were volatile. Sixth, he listed "secret prayer" as a key part of his success. Finally, he incorporated "wit and wisdom" in his sermons by telling parables and stories his White and Black listeners readily connected with.[3]

Seven Men

This chapter argues that seven men—four White men and three Black men—profoundly helped make Marshall Keeble the church planter he became. First, the Black evangelist credited David Lipscomb (1831–1917) with lighting a "fire" under African Americans in Churches of Christ. Through the pages of the *Gospel Advocate*, Lipscomb left a lasting imprint on Keeble and the many congregations he planted. The White editor perhaps more than any other person helped to lead Keeble's father-in-law out of the Disciples of Christ into Churches of Christ. A year after Lipscomb passed away, Keeble reported, "So I am still reading [the *Gospel Advocate*]. May God bless and lead those in whose hands the paper is to remain, and may it go forth blessing the world as it did when that great and noble servant, David Lipscomb, lived."[4]

Second, N. B. Hardeman (1874–1965), a renowned preacher and educator in White Churches of Christ, met Keeble in 1918 in Henderson, Tennessee. When angry Black religionists in Henderson denied Keeble access to their building, Hardeman helped him secure a place to preach. Keeble testified, "On the last night Brother N. B. Hardeman and others came out and made remarks in the meeting. This was my first time to meet Brother Hardeman, and, in my judgment, he is a fine, Christian man."[5] Through Hardeman's efforts, Keeble went on to plant his first congregation, the Oak Grove Church of Christ, in Henderson in 1918.

Third, Joe McPherson (1862–1918), a White "mail-carrier preacher," left an indelible mark on Keeble's preaching and theology. In 1914, McPherson conducted a "protracted meeting" in Nashville for one month. Keeble never forgot this campaign, stating, "I copied every lesson Brother McPherson preached; and though he is dead, I am still preaching his sermons, and these lessons are still bringing men to Christ." Two years after McPherson's death, Keeble acknowledged, "Although Brother Joe McPherson has gone from us, his labors and his influence among us still live." He then added that McPherson "did more toward teaching me how to preach than any man I ever heard."[6]

How exactly did Joe McPherson influence Keeble's preaching? In a 1915 article, "Baptized to Obey the Lord," McPherson rehearsed his conversion in the Baptist church, noting that he went to an "unscriptural mourner's bench," related an "unscriptural experience," made an "unscriptural confession," submitted to an "unscriptural vote," and was baptized for an "unscriptural purpose and into an unscriptural organization." But after being thoroughly convinced that baptism was "for the remission of sins," McPherson abandoned the Baptist church and received baptism into Churches of Christ. Thus, he concluded, "You owe it to yourself and to the one seeking the truth. Bear in mind that it is impossible for an unscriptural faith to produce a scriptural obedience."[7]

Everywhere Keeble preached he denounced the mourners' bench and echoed the same tenet that baptism is for the remission of sins; thus, Baptists, Methodists, and other believers must be rebaptized to become members of Churches of Christ. When preaching in Valdosta, Georgia, in 1931, Keeble proclaimed a message similar to Joe McPherson's. "I want to say just here," affirmed Keeble, "that the baptism the Bible talks about and the one Ananias told Saul to submit to was for the purpose of washing away sins. And you all been saying that your sins was pardoned at the mourners' bench." He then added, "Brother Methodist and Brother Baptist, friends, get a sinner down here on the mourners' bench and they all circle around him, stay there all night trying to get him through." After condemning religious groups who called seekers to the mourners' bench, Keeble said there was a simpler way, a New Testament way: Urge them to be "buried with Christ in baptism for the remission of sins."[8] Then sinners could have confidence immediately in their saved status and go on their way rejoicing.

Fourth, Alexander Campbell (1862–1930), a fiery Black preacher, led S. W. Womack (1851–1920) and Marshall Keeble out of the Gay Street Christian Church. In 1918, Keeble wrote, "It was these two men [Campbell and Womack] that encouraged me to preach the gospel, and I shall never be through praising them and thanking God for such blessings. . . . Brother Womack and Brother

Campbell say that the *Gospel Advocate* has been second with them, and the Bible first."[9]

But fifth, S. W. Womack, Keeble's father-in-law, without question had the greatest impact on his development as a gospel preacher. In the 1880s, Womack preached across the mid-South and contributed articles to the *Christian Standard*. When preaching in Nashville, Tennessee, in 1882, he praised the organist, Miss Calhoun, for "faithfully [doing] her part in making good music."[10] Yet within a decade, Womack had shifted his attention from Isaac Errett and the *Christian Standard*, a leading voice among the Disciples of Christ, to David Lipscomb and the *Gospel Advocate*. Keeble observed that Womack delighted visiting the "*Gospel Advocate* office, because, he said, he was always made welcome by the whole staff. Whenever he got puzzled over any passage of Scripture, he would always have a conference with old Brother David Lipscomb during his life time."[11]

Keeble later confessed, "I am a young preacher endeavoring to make a success in life, and if I can just make the man that Brother Womack is, I will be thankful. His success in life, in a material way, has not been very great, but I have reference to the great treasures he is laying up in heaven." More specifically, Keeble inherited from his father-in-law a high ecclesiology. In 1902, when controversial innovations engulfed African Americans in the Stone–Campbell Movement, Womack asserted, "We have no entertainments, no clubs, no ladies' aid societies; but we believe in meeting these obligations through the church, the God-given institution provided for all his work."[12] Decades later, Keeble extolled the Church of Christ above all other religious groups. In the 1950s, he preached, "It is his church and his church should wear his name. When we become members of this church we need not worry, for we know that it will never be rooted up." Christ's church, he added, was "blood bought, rock bottom and Holy Ghost filled. Thank God."[13]

Sixth, A. M. Burton (1879–1965), a wealthy White entrepreneur and devout Christian, funded the preaching efforts of several Black preachers. Alonzo Jones, a Black preacher in Chattanooga, Tennessee, noted that the White benefactor "remembered me with the value of sixty dollars as a contribution to me in my work for the Master."[14] But Burton reserved his most generous support for Marshall Keeble. When traveling to the nation's capital, Keeble announced, "Brother A. M. Burton has agreed to pay my railroad fare here, round trip, for which I am very thankful." In 1925, the Black preacher heaped more praise on the White philanthropist: "Brother Burton for years has helped me in my work. I have never had to ask him to help me in my work; he just sees what I am trying to do." He then explained, "To my mind, Brother A. M. Burton is the greatest missionary in the church to-day. If it were not for him, much of my work would have to go undone."[15]

Seventh, Booker T. Washington (1856–1915), esteemed educator of Tuskegee Institute, also left an imprint on Keeble, who confessed to having read *Up from Slavery* "from lid to lid." According to biographer J. E. Choate (1916–2013), Keeble "learned from Booker T. Washington what he couldn't learn from the Bible. By that, Keeble meant he learned to respect his race, to hold a high opinion of himself, and especially how to get along with white people."[16] In essence, Keeble learned not to "rock the boat" of race relations across the South. Therefore, when White seekers in the South responded to his preaching, he often allowed the White church leaders to baptize the White candidates who requested it. Keeble clearly understood a White person submitting to a Black man for baptism would be an affront in the Jim Crow South.

In conclusion, Marshall Keeble was not a self-made man. Several people helped to mold and shape his preaching life. David Lipscomb, through the pages of the *Gospel Advocate*, furnished him a working knowledge of Scripture and a theological framework for reading it. Joe McPherson taught him the art of sermon construction and how to impart biblical information. N. B. Hardeman opened up doors to help him plant his first congregation in Henderson, Tennessee. S. W. Womack and Alexander Campbell led him out of the Christian Church and molded his "hard" preaching style and his high ecclesiology. A. M. Burton generally funded his preaching campaigns, and Booker T. Washington trained him how to navigate the boisterous waters of racial conflict in the segregated South.

NOTES

[1]J. E. Choate, *Roll Jordan Roll: A Biography of Marshall Keeble* (Gospel Advocate, 1974), xiii.

[2]Kidada E. Williams, *I Saw Death Coming: A History of Terror and Survival in the War against Reconstruction* (Bloomsbury, 2023), xi.

[3]Robinson, *Show Us How You Do It*, 2.

[4]Marshall Keeble, "Among the Colored Folks," *Gospel Advocate* 60 (Feb. 14, 1918): 163.

[5]Robinson, *Show Us How You Do It*, 15.

[6]Keeble, "Among the Colored Folks," *Gospel Advocate* 62 (May 27, 1920): 532; Keeble, "Among the Colored Folks," *Gospel Advocate* 63 (Sept. 15, 1921): 911. See also Robinson, *Show Us How You Do It*, 16.

[7]Joe McPherson, "Baptized to Obey the Lord," *The Open Arena* 11 (Jan. 1915): 2.

[8]B. C. Goodpasture, ed., *Biography and Sermons of Marshall Keeble, Evangelist* (Gospel Advocate, 1952 [1931]), 79–80.

[9]Keeble, "Among the Colored Folks" *Gospel Advocate* 60 (Feb. 14, 1918): 163.

[10]S. W. Womack, "Our Colored Brethren," *Christian Standard* 17 (Apr. 18, 1882): 107.

[11]Cited in Robinson, *Show Us How You Do It*, 17.

[12]Cited in Robinson, *Show Us How You Do It*, 17.

[13]Robinson, *Show Us How You Do It*, 60.

[14]Robinson, *Show Us How You Do It*, 25.

[15]Robinson, *Show Us How You Do It*, 26.

[16]Choate, *Roll Jordan Roll*, 21.

PART TWO

MARSHALL KEEBLE

His Life and Ministry

CHAPTER FOUR

THE EARLY YEARS

John Mark Hicks

Marshall Keeble's early ministry reflected the values, practices, and hopes of his father-in-law, Samuel W. Womack.[1] When Womack died in 1920, Keeble vowed to continue his legacy and "imitate the Christian life he [had] left behind." Although Jesus Christ was the pattern for godly living, as a "young preacher," Keeble endeavored "to make a success in life" by becoming "the man that Brother Womack is."[2]

This chapter explores how Marshall Keeble's early years both continued and extended the ministry of his most intimate mentor. After a brief description of his early life and evangelistic efforts, I identify four key areas in which Keeble followed Womack's example. Those commitments remained constant in Keeble's fifty-four year ministry as an evangelist and educator.

Early Biography

When asked by a reporter for *The Tennessean* in 1964 why he became a preacher, Keeble quipped that he grew up "in a nest of preachers," which "made it a natural thing for me to do." He was not exaggerating. Keeble's enslaved grandfather began holding revivals before the Civil War. As the personal valet of Major Horace Pinkney Keeble, a prominent lawyer in Murfreesboro, Tennessee, he could read and write. "The white Keebles were Church of Christ people," and thus Robert Keeble "stayed with the church."[3] After the war, he continued to preach, and his young grandson, Marshall, sometimes attended his meetings. Marshall's uncle, also named Marshall Keeble, began preaching while enslaved and served as an evangelist for forty years throughout Tennessee and neighboring states. In an interview in 1967, Keeble remembered his uncle's preaching as full of Scripture quotations and his style as "pretty rapid and pretty exact, strict and fine." "I have mighty near," he commented, "the same style he had."[4]

Marshall Keeble was born to Robert and Mittie Keeble on December 7, 1878, in Rutherford County, Tennessee; his parents, formerly enslaved, "sharecropped on the hilly slopes of the farm." The Keebles moved to Nashville in 1882. After Preston Taylor became the minister of the Gay Street Christian Church, Robert worked in his funeral business and assisted with the church. Eventually, Taylor established the Lea Avenue Christian Church in 1891. Taylor baptized Marshall Keeble in October 1892 when he was thirteen.[5]

Keeble's seventh-grade education served him well. In Mrs. Gowey's class from the fourth through seventh grades, he regularly memorized speeches and poetry for classroom recitation and speech giving. Keeble was quite competitive and wanted to be the best.[6]

Marshall's future father-in-law, Samuel W. Womack, was a member of the Gay Street Christian Church. In 1897, Marshall married Minnie Womack, and the Womacks boarded with the Keebles for a period of time.[7] Minnie was a graduate of the High School Department at Fisk University. According to Marshall, Minnie was "his best teacher," as she schooled him in grammar, reading, and writing, and, according to Keeble, she often led "the song service" when she traveled with him.[8]

In his teens, Keeble clerked in a grocery store and worked in a soap factory. In his twenties, he opened a store on Hamilton Street and then opened a second one on Jefferson Street in 1907. His sister-in-law Philistia operated the Hamilton store, while Minnie ran the Jefferson store. Keeble himself worked out of a huckster wagon on the streets of downtown Nashville. The *Nashville Globe* contained advertisements for what was called "Marshall Keebles Bros., Groceries, Wood and Coal. Our Motto: Honesty and Quality" at "2005 Jefferson St., near 19th Ave."[9]

Keeble was also an active leader in the church at Jackson Street, including serving as church treasurer. He also began to preach. In the *Tennessean* interview, he said, "I was just eighteen when I delivered my first sermon at the Jackson Street Church of Christ right here in Nashville." But he did not preach regularly for several years. According to his interview with Forrest Roads, he first started "making talks" in a training class and then at midweek prayer services. Reflecting on his experience at the beginnings of Jackson Street, he recalled that he "was trained as a Christian worker" there, "doing anything that I was asked to do by my older brethren" (including Womack). In those early days, his mother-in-law, "Aunt Sallie," said Marshall "would never make a preacher," although by the end of her life, she insisted Marshall preach whenever he was at Jackson Street on a Sunday.[10]

The earliest documented example, to my knowledge, of Keeble preaching is during a two-week meeting in August–September 1903 when Keeble and Womack assisted Thomas Harris. Eventually, when Womack would speak on a Sunday morning at Jackson Street, Keeble would often speak at the evening service.[11] In addition, throughout the first decade of the twentieth century, he regularly preached at the three Nashville missions. He participated in tent preaching, for example, at the corner of Hamilton and Park streets in June 1906, where he aided Womack in exhorting everyone "to take the bible as our counsel." On another occasion, Womack reported that Keeble "preached for the East Nashville Mission, on Crutcher Street, at three o'clock, with a large hearing" in November 1908.[12]

He also served communities outside of Nashville as an occasional preacher. On May 21, 1908, he "preached for the little band at Dozier's Schoolhouse" in Davidson County. In 1908, he conducted what some believe was his first protracted meeting at Center Star near Centerville, Tennessee, for eight days and baptized twenty-five. He often traveled with Alexander Campbell. They were in Hickman County on June 23, 1912, at the Air Rock meetinghouse and returned in August–September for an eight-day meeting, where eleven were baptized and fifteen restored.[13]

His early work was recognized in the African American city paper *Nashville Globe*. It reported that in September 1911, "there was a large crowd out at Center Station Sunday. Mr. Marshall Keeble, of Nashville," along with Dennis English, preached, and "their sermons were highly enjoyed by all." Keeble also preached at Pleasant Union and Air Rock meetinghouses. "He did a great and grand work," including at least seven baptisms, the paper reported.[14]

An Evangelist

Following in the footsteps of his mentors, S. W. Womack and Alexander Campbell, Keeble began full-time evangelistic work in 1914. They had both "encouraged" him "to preach the gospel and I shall never be through praising and thanking God for such blessings." In his only report in the *Gospel Advocate* during his first two years, on November 11, 1915, he wrote, "For the last two years I have given up everything in order to carry the gospel."[15] He preached in many of the same places Womack had cultivated in previous years but also worked in new fields. From July to October of 1915, for example, he was at Center Star and Air Rock in Hickman County, Capeleville in Shelby County, Philadelphia in Loudon County, Dyersburg and Newbern in Dyer County, Bell Buckle in Bedford County, Jackson Street in Nashville, Lebanon in Wilson County, and Viola and McMinnville in Warren County. Keeble would return to these same places several times over the next decade while expanding his reach into new places.

Center Star in Hickman County illustrates what was typical for Keeble in those early years of evangelistic ministry. "Keeble would ride the train to Centerville from where he would walk the last remaining twelve miles to Center Star." Traveling with a Bible and a hemp sack, he would return home with "a couple of rabbits, a hen, and maybe some molasses. After the meeting Keeble would put the sack on his shoulder and hike through the darkness to catch the train back to Nashville."[16]

Two places illustrate Keeble's early evangelistic ministry. On October 3, 1915, Keeble began a five-day meeting at Bell Buckle in Bedford County, Tennessee. He had been invited by W. R. Mingle, a local White leader. "There were only four black members," and they did not assemble regularly. During the meeting, two were baptized and another added to the congregation. Mingle described Keeble as "a forceful speaker [who] presented the gospel in its primitive simplicity."[17] The following year in May, Keeble returned to conduct what he called "the greatest meeting I ever conducted" in a full schoolhouse. Three were baptized. Keeble was there again in the summer of 1917 for ten days with one baptism. The White and Black congregations decided to purchase a "place of worship." Keeble expressed appreciation for the White church that had "done so much to help reach my people with the gospel at this place."[18]

When Keeble returned in 1918, he found "between twenty and twenty-five there, worshipping in the schoolhouse," and Mingle met with them regularly, "trying to teach them how to keep house for the Lord." Keeble held his sixth meeting with the group later that spring, and then another meeting in the fall. In 1919, he held his eighth meeting in five years at Bell Buckle.[19] During those five years, the congregation took root, grew to a membership in the twenties, and constructed a meetinghouse with the help of the White congregation. This illustrates how Keeble invested in "destitute fields" as mission points even if the results were not spectacular.

Chester County, Tennessee, offers a different kind of example. For three months in 1917 (February through April), Keeble visited "congregations and mission points" in West Tennessee, Arkansas, and Mississippi. His last stop before returning home was Henderson, Tennessee, where he "remained two nights, preaching in [the] private home" of Bose Crooms, and three were baptized.[20] In July–August 1918, Keeble conducted a three-week meeting in Henderson. Eighty-four people were baptized—"all from the sects"—and this group planted a church in Henderson. "The white Christians did all they could to assist us in the meeting," and "on the last night Brother N. B. Hardeman and others came out and made remarks in the meeting." In the fall of 1918, he stopped over in Henderson and baptized six more during a brief stay and returned in 1919, where he found over one hundred worshiping together and preparing to build a meetinghouse.[21]

These two congregations illustrated Keeble's desire to preach the gospel in "destitute places" and his commitment to care for these churches by returning multiple times over their beginning years. These mission points saw new congregations established, growth in numbers, and a new meetinghouse erected. Although the numbers were greater in Henderson, Keeble gave much more attention to Bell Buckle.

Keeble often summarized his annual efforts. His goal, he wrote, was to "preach the gospel to my people." Yet, "if it had not been for the aid given by the white people, I would have suffered, and I am so thankful for such kind and Christian fellowship." In January 1919, he summarized four of his first five years of full-time evangelistic ministry.[22]

Year	Sermons	Baptisms	Restored	Miles Traveled
1915	240	90	23	5,260
1916	335	135	30	5,000
1917	297	104	16	6,497
1918	219	128	17	6,295
Total	**1,161**	**457**	**86**	**23,052**

Four Shared Commitments

First, Womack and Keeble shared a common commitment to the work of itinerant preaching, which included nurturing existing congregations, planting new ones in destitute fields, and holding protracted meetings among African Americans with the aid—although sometimes without the aid—of White congregations. Womack was first a school teacher in Fosterville, Tennessee, and had been active in the Restoration Movement since his baptism in 1866. He attended church consultation gatherings and was in regular communication with David Lipscomb. He moved to Nashville in the early 1880s and began full-time evangelistic work in October 1883. Womack wanted to focus on new mission points while, at the same time, nurturing churches for which he cared in the counties surrounding Nashville. Marshall's travels with Womack and Campbell gave him, according to Smith, "a pattern for the rest of his career."[23]

Second, Womack and Keeble shared a common respect and admiration for Booker T. Washington, which shaped their understanding of race relations and how they approached White Christians for help in their ministries. In the year Washington died, Womack quoted the educator and named him as "one of our great and useful men."[24] Keeble heard Washington speak at the Ryman in Nashville several times. Washington, Keeble said in an interview, had "done a lot to help me." As Choate notes, "Keeble knew *Up From Slavery* from lid to lid."[25] According to Rhoads, Keeble learned "respect for his race, to hold a high opinion of himself, how to get along with white people, and how to get financial support from white people." Keeble said, "White brethren often speak to me, 'You're better than Booker T. Washington. You draw more people than he did.' . . . And when I see these audiences everywhere I go now, he comes in my mind."[26]

In 1915, after years of segregation, Womack remembered the cordiality of a White congregation that served the "wine and bread" in a more inclusive manner than what he presently experienced. He complained that often "white brethren . . . do but little or nothing toward helping" them. The "brethren," he argued, "need to give this help to develop and strengthen their spiritual character more than the preacher needs it."[27]

Robinson's work explores the imbalance of power and systemic racism that were often part of these relationships, including paternalism and assimilation as well as segregation.[28] Keeble was sometimes loved because he knew how, in the words of one White brother, to stay in his place. But Keeble's humility, although genuine, "was founded on the bravado of Brer Rabbit, who in countless slave tales outwits the Fox and the Bear by pitting his weakness against their strength."[29]

Third, Womack and Keeble shared a common conservative theology that opposed innovations in the apostolic order (including fundraising festivals, instrumental music, and missionary societies). They conducted their evangelistic work through the church rather than through parachurch organizations.

By the late 1890s, Womack was working closely with a Black itinerant evangelist by the name of Alexander Cleveland Campbell, who had been baptized by Marshall Keeble's uncle—D. M. Keeble—and attended Lea Avenue Christian Church. Womack and Campbell conducted meetings together in Nashville and other places.[30] Campbell was increasingly uncomfortable with the use of instrumental music at Lea Avenue and its participation in missionary societies, both of which were "innovations" contrary to "pure worship" according to "apostolic" doctrine. The final straw was the use of denominational preachers when Preston Taylor was away. In around 1900, Campbell withdrew from Lea Avenue and began meeting in his own "rented house in the city" with his immediate family.[31] Within the next few months, he persuaded S. W. Womack and Marshall Keeble to join him, and Womack withdrew from the Gay Street congregation. They "continued together" in Campbell's home until they could make further arrangements for a meetinghouse.[32]

In 1914, Campbell was pleased with the "fruits of withdrawing from the digressive colored churches and of [his] labors on apostolic grounds." Jackson Street became the "mother" of African American Churches of Christ in Middle Tennessee and beyond.[33] According to Womack, they started a mission point on the corner of Jackson and Watkins streets in Northwest Nashville on January 6, 1901. This was a community that preferred "the old way in the work and worship of the church." They raised funds through free-will offerings. "We have no entertainments," Womack wrote. "No clubs, no ladies' aid societies; but we believe in meeting these obligations through the church, the God-given institution provided for all his work."[34]

Womack was strongly influenced by David Lipscomb and the *Gospel Advocate*. He was mostly supported by the *Advocate* constituency, and he had been an avid reader of the magazine since 1866. Keeble's grandfather was also an avid reader.[35] Moreover, Womack regularly consulted with Lipscomb at the *Gospel Advocate* office, where they would study the Bible together for hours. "When he got puzzled over any passage of scripture, he would always have a conference with old Brother Lipscomb," Keeble remembered.[36] Lipscomb actively encouraged the leaders of Jackson Street "to press on, and they did," Keeble noted. Indeed, J. M. McCaleb, after speaking at Jackson Street in 1911, recounted that some unnamed White brother had remarked, "Brother Womack is to the colored people what Brother Lipscomb is to the white people."[37]

Keeble also remained committed to the evangelistic work that was unencumbered by societies and parachurch organizations. As he entered his fourth year of work, he remarked, "I have been asked a number of times by brethren who favor the plan the 'digressives' have to support the evangelist, how I am supported, and my answer is, God will provide; for in the commission of

Christ promises to be with the one who will faithfully carry the message and I had rather rely on God's plan than man's."[38]

Fourth, Womack and Keeble shared a common commitment to Christian education. They both started a new school at Jackson Street and both served on the board of trustees for the Silver Point Christian Institute. Both saw the need for an educated people, especially a trained ministry. Womack himself was concerned about this as far back as a church consultation in Franklin, Tennessee, in 1882 where African American leaders gathered to discuss the needs of both an "educated ministry" and the "work of an evangelist," among a few other items.[39]

In 1905, Alexander Campbell, G. P. Bowser (a graduate of Walden University), and S. W. Womack (a former school teacher) gathered at Jackson Street to discuss, among other things, "school work." According to Womack, David Lipscomb "was the first to mention" to him the establishment of a school like the Nashville Bible School for African Americans.[40] The school opened on October 7, 1907, at the Jackson Street Church of Christ under the leadership of G. P. Bowser, with Philistia Womack as a full-time teacher. The curriculum included the daily study of the Bible. The school moved to Silver Point, Tennessee, in 1909 but closed in 1920. Womack served on the board of trustees and as a teacher. By 1916, Marshall Keeble was also serving on the board.[41]

These four commitments remained constant in Keeble's fifty-four-year ministry as an evangelist and educator. He never wavered, and his impact, by God's grace, formed communities ready for every good work.

NOTES

[1]Biographical details are primarily based on Robinson, *Show Us How You Do It*, 11–13; George Barker, "Brother Keeble and the Lord," *Nashville Tennessee Magazine* (Mar. 29, 1964): 6–7, 15; Forrest Neil Rhoads, "A Study of the Sources of Marshall Keeble's Effectiveness as a Preacher" (PhD dissertation, Southern Illinois University, 1970); and J. E. Choate, *Roll Jordan Roll: A Biography of Marshall Keeble* (Gospel Advocate, 1968), 14–17. Substantive studies of Marshall Keeble are: Robinson, "'The Two Old Heroes': Samuel W. Womack, Alexander Campbell and the Origins of Black Churches of Christ in the United States," *Discipliana* 65, no. 1 (Spring 2005): 3–20; Paul D. Phillips, "The Interracial Impact of Marshall Keeble Black Evangelist, 1878–1968," *Tennessee Historical Quarterly* 36, no. 1 (Spring 1977): 62–74; Darrell L. Broking, "Marshall Keeble and the Implementation of a Grand Strategy" (MA thesis, East Tennessee State University, 2003); and Arthur Lee Smith Jr., "A Rhetorical Analysis of the Speaking of Marshall Keeble" (MA thesis, Pepperdine University, 1965).

[2]Keeble, "A Great Man Gone," *Gospel Advocate* 62, no. 29 (July 29, 1920): 745; Keeble, "Things That We Should Be Thankful For," *Gospel Advocate* 60, no. 7 (Feb. 14, 1918): 163.

[3]Barker, "Brother Keeble and the Lord," 6–7, 15.

[4]Rhoads, "Sources," 65–66.

[5]Smith, "Rhetorical Analysis," 20; Keeble, "News and Notes," *Gospel Advocate* 84, no. 38 (Sept. 17, 1942): 907. In "Thankful," 162, Keeble says "fourteen."

[6]Rhoads, "Sources," 70–71.

[7]Their marriage license was issued in December 1897; *The Tennessean* (Dec. 13, 1897), 3; Robinson, "'The Two Old Heroes,'" 5; and Robinson, *Show Us How You Do It*, 13.

[8]In "At Fisk University," *Nashville American* (June 12, 1895): 8, Minnie is two years away from completing the course for teachers. She finished in June 1897; *The Tennessean* (June 16, 1897), 6. "[B]est teacher" comes from Choate, *Roll Jordan Roll*, 18. Keeble, "Brother Keeble's Report," *Gospel Advocate* 58, no. 25 (June 22, 1916): 638 ("She leads the song service"); and Keeble, "Among the Colored Folks," *Gospel Advocate* 60, no. 35 (Aug. 29, 1918): 835 ("she is a great help in leading the song service").

[9]Choate, *Roll Jordan Roll*, 17, 19; *Nashville Globe* (Apr. 17, 1908), 5; see also *Nashville Globe* (May 1, 1908), 5.

[10]Womack, "Work among the Colored People," *Gospel Advocate* 51, no. 11 (Mar. 18, 1909): 341; Barker, "Brother Keeble," 6; Keeble, "Among the Colored People: Annual Report," *Gospel Advocate* 59, no. 4 (Jan. 25, 1917): 93; Choate, *Roll Jordan Roll*, 22.

[11]Womack, "Work among the Colored People," *Gospel Advocate* 48, no. 40 (Oct. 1, 1918): 639; Womack, "Work among the Colored People," *Gospel Advocate* 50, no. 47 (Nov. 21, 1912): 1276; Womack, "Report of Work Done," *Gospel Advocate* 55, no. 40 (Oct. 2, 1913): 958.

[12]Womack, "Work among the Colored People," *Gospel Advocate* 50, no. 50 (Dec. 10, 1908): 797; Womack, "Tent Meeting," *Gospel Advocate* 48, no. 25 (June 21, 1906): 397.

[13] Womack, "Work among the Colored People," *Gospel Advocate* 50, no. 25 (June 18, 1908): 395; Choate, *Roll Jordan Roll*, 35; A. B. Lipscomb, "Cheerful Messages," *Gospel Advocate* 54, no. 37 (Sept. 12, 1912): 1028.

[14] "Duck River Notes," *Nashville Globe* (Sept. 29, 1911): 2.

[15] Keeble, "Thankful For," 162; Keeble, "Among the Colored People," *Gospel Advocate* 57, no. 45 (Nov. 11, 1915): 1150–51.

[16] Barker, "Brother Keeble," 15.

[17] W. R. Mingle, "The Master's Vineyard," *Gospel Advocate* 57, no. 42 (Oct. 21, 1915): 1063; also Keeble, "Among the Colored People," *Gospel Advocate* 57, no. 45 (Nov. 11, 1915): 1151.

[18] Keeble, "Report of M. Keeble," *Gospel Advocate* 59, no. 44 (Nov. 1, 1917): 1066.

[19] Keeble, "Brother Keeble's Report," *Gospel Advocate* 58, no. 25 (June 22, 1916): 638; Mingle, "Tennessee," *Gospel Advocate* 59, no. 28 (July 12, 1917): 687; Keeble, "Report of M. Keeble," *Gospel Advocate* 59, no. 44 (Nov. 1, 1917): 1066.

[20] Keeble, "Brother M. Keeble's Report," *Gospel Advocate* 59, no. 19 (May 10, 1917): 471.

[21] Keeble, "Among the Colored Folks: Sowing and Reaping," *Gospel Advocate* 60, no. 37 (Sept. 12, 1918): 879; Keeble, "Among the Colored Folks," *Gospel Advocate* 60, no. 51 (Dec. 18, 1918): 1222; Keeble, "An Interesting Report," *Gospel Advocate* 61, no. 24 (June 12, 1919): 572.

[22] Keeble, "Four Years of Evangelistic Work," *Gospel Advocate* 61, no. 2 (Jan. 9, 1919): 41.

[23] *Republican Banner* (Nov. 18, 1874): 4; and Lipscomb, "Items, Personal, Etc.," *Gospel Advocate* 18, no. 4 (Jan. 27, 1876): 98. He was still living in Fosterville, Tennessee, when he submitted a note to the *Gospel Advocate*; Lipscomb, "Items, Personal, Etc.," *Gospel Advocate* 22, no. 17 (April 22, 1880): 267. Womack, "Among the Colored People: Attitude of the Races," *Gospel Advocate* 57, no. 52 (Dec, 30, 1915): 1326. Marshall Keeble numbered his years of ministry as "forty," cf. Keeble, "Great Man," 745; Womack, "Editorial Brevities," *Gospel Advocate* 25, no. 46 (Nov. 14, 1883): 727.

[24] Robinson, *Show Us How You Do It*, 28, 34, 97; Womack, "Attitude of the Races," 1326.

[25] Choate, *Roll Jordan Roll*, 21.

[26] Rhoads, "Sources," 78, 80.

[27] Lipscomb, "Missionary Work," *Gospel Advocate* 44, no. 43 (Oct. 23, 1902): 681.

[28] See Robinson, "'The Two Old Heroes,'" 7–10, and Robinson, *Hard-Fighting Soldiers: A History of African American Churches of Christ* (University of Tennessee Press, 2019), especially 33–54. See also Phillips, "Interracial Impact of Marshall Keeble," 62–74, and Broking, "Grand Strategy."

[29] J. W. Brents, "Sowing and Reaping," *Gospel Advocate* 73, no. 42 (Oct. 15, 1931): 1289 ("He knows his place and at all times scrupulously keeps it"). Don Haymes, "Keeble, Marshall," in *The Encyclopedia of the Stone-Campbell Movement*, eds. Douglas Foster et al. (Eerdmans, 2004), 441.

[30] Womack, "The Growth of the Word," *Gospel Advocate* 40, no. 32 (Aug. 11, 1898): 513; Womack, "The Growth of the Word," *Gospel Advocate* 40, no. 39 (Sept. 29, 1898): 624.

[31]W. W. Brightwell, "News and Notes," *Gospel Advocate* 78, no. 10 (Mar. 5, 1936): 235, says around 1898, and within two years they erected a building. That squares with the beginnings of the Jackson Street church in 1900 in Campbell's house.

[32]Alexander Campbell, "Work among the Colored People," *Gospel Advocate* 51, no. 48 (Dec. 2, 1909): 1523; Campbell, "Among the Colored People: Jackson Street Mission," *Gospel Advocate* 56, no. 15 (Apr. 9, 1914): 414.

[33]Campbell, "Among the Colored People: Jackson Street," 414; "Keeble to Be Here," *Gospel Advocate* 61, no. 52 (Dec. 1941): 1242 ("the mother church among the colored people").

[34]Womack, "Church News," *Gospel Advocate* 43, no. 41 (Oct. 10, 1901): 653; Campbell, "Among the Colored People," *Gospel Advocate* 59, no. 8 (Feb. 22, 1917): 186; Womack, "Church News," *Gospel Advocate* 44, no. 15 (Apr. 10, 1902): 237.

[35]Womack, "Church News," 43, no. 41: 653; Keeble, "Thankful For," 162.

[36]Keeble, "Great Man Gone," 745; cf. also Womack, "Among the Colored People," *Gospel Advocate* 60, no. 1 (Jan. 3, 1918): 1326 ("So many times I have met him at the office, and any part of the Book that I did not understand, he was ready to help me out on it").

[37]Keeble, "Work Among Our Colored Brethren," *Gospel Advocate* 67, no. 5 (Jan. 29, 1926): 117; J. M. McCaleb, "Missionary," *Gospel Advocate* 53, no. 3 (Jan. 19, 1911): 75.

[38]Keeble, "Evangelistic Work for Three Years," *Gospel Advocate* 60, no. 5 (Jan. 31, 1918): 115. See Robinson, *Hard-Fighting*, 57–71.

[39]H. S. Berry, "The Consultation at Franklin," *Gospel Advocate* 24, no. 37 (Sept. 14, 1882): 584.

[40]Womack, "Church News," *Gospel Advocate* 47, no. 39 (Sept. 28, 1905): 620; Womack, "Among the Colored Folk," *Gospel Advocate* 60, no. 1 (Jan. 3, 1918): 18.

[41]Womack, "Church News," *Gospel Advocate* 49, no. 41 (Oct. 10, 1907): 655; E. A. Elam, "Help the Colored People," *Gospel Advocate* 53, no. 7 (Feb. 16, 1911): 206; "Report of Silver Point Bible School for Negroes," *Gospel Advocate* 58, no. 30 (July 27, 1916): 748–49.

CHAPTER FIVE

HIS PREACHING LIFE

Edward J. Robinson

In 1914, the same year World War I began, Marshall Keeble committed his life to full-time evangelism. At the start of his evangelistic career, African American Churches of Christ were a fledgling fellowship. Annie C. Tuggle (1890–1976) reported that she had to read Scripture in worship for a Black preacher because there were "no men able to help him."[1] Illiteracy and incapacity marked the existence of the handful of Black Churches of Christ in the opening decades of the twentieth century. Therefore, three years later, Keeble announced, "I have given up all that I might preach the gospel to my people."[2]

Sacrifice, Selflessness, and Suffering

Sacrifice, selflessness, and suffering marked Keeble's preaching life. Indeed, the African American evangelist faced many struggles as he traversed the United States preaching what he believed to be the "pure gospel."[3]

In the first decades of the twentieth century, Marshall Keeble often spent many months away from his family. In 1921, he reported, "I have been away from my family now about three months, and I yet have one more meeting to hold before I can be blessed with seeing them again."[4] His extended absences attested not only to his devotion to the cause of Christ, but they also spoke to his wife's patience and support of his work. This perhaps explains why Keeble attributed his evangelistic success to his wife, Minnie Womack (1880–1933), whom he said was at the "bottom of his preaching career."[5] A daughter of Samuel W. Womack (1851–1920) and Sallie Womack, Minnie completed her studies in the High School Department at Fisk University in Nashville, Tennessee. Since Marshall Keeble never finished the seventh grade, his wife compensated for many educational shortcomings her husband might have had. Indeed, Keeble often confessed that "marrying into the Womack family was one of the great blessings of his life."[6]

Minnie was truly a great blessing to her husband, but his greatest supporter became a major source of grief when she passed away in 1933, in the early years of the Great Depression. Keeble expressed gratitude to his supporters, stating, "I want to thank my many friends for the comforting messages that were sent me, after my dear wife passed away, leaving me very lonely; but I mean to hold to God's unchanging hand, so I can meet her in the sweet by and by."[7] Three years later, Keeble suffered more tragedies when his mother, Mittie, passed away at age seventy-five. Additionally, two of his children died in infancy. A son, Clarence, died at age ten after being electrocuted. His daughter, Beatrice, passed away in 1935; and his son Robert expired in 1964. Keeble, then, survived his first wife and all five of his children. Yet, these deep losses, coupled with the cloud of the economic distress engendered by the Great Depression, failed to deter him from doing God's work.

What kept Keeble trudging amid such difficult circumstances? His favorite song perhaps provides insight into the source of his strength: "Hold to God's Unchanging Hand." The first stanza went:

> Time is filled with swift transition,
> Naught of earth unmoved shall stand,
> Build your hopes on things eternal,
> Hold to God's unchanging hand![8]

Published in 1904, this hymn urged Christians to focus on "heav'nly treasures" and "not on this world's vain riches." Such lyrics helped steer Keeble away from worldly pursuits and even political issues, and his concentration on "things eternal" doubtlessly empowered him to soldier on in the face of such adversity and affliction.

Potent Gifts

Even though Keeble faced many hard challenges, he also possessed certain potent and priceless gifts. First, he displayed an unshakable commitment to the "pure gospel" and an unwavering faith in God. Second, he had a diverse cast of strong White and Black Christians standing behind him. Third, he had the uncanny ability to preach parabolic sermons, marked by humor, simplicity, and sincerity. One of his former students argued, "Keeble's ability to appear simple in style, yet sincere, made him the first popular Negro preacher for the churches of Christ."[9] Another student of Keeble's preaching has observed that his "effectiveness as a tent evangelist was based on his disarming humor, giving him access to all types of audiences."[10] Forrest Neil Rhoads, a former communications professor at Lipscomb University, has pointed out that Keeble "understood human nature, especially that of the members of his own race, and he used logical proof well, specifically in

Marshall Keeble's first wife, Minnie, died in 1932, and he married Laura Johnson (pictured here) in 1934.

appealing to the Bible, in using his enthymeme 'the Bible is right,' and in his parables and personal experiences."[11]

Willie Cato (1923–91), a close associate and traveling companion of Keeble's, observed that Keeble was "no superman. He was very human. His faith and confidence in God and in His Word committed Marshall Keeble to always 'see the hand of God' when he preached. He knew the power was in the Word, not in the man." In Cato's view, Keeble mastered the art of using common illustrations to teach biblical principles. "Often he assured the audience," explained Cato, "that a piece of bread out of a white man's hand and a black man's hand has the same ingredients. It's the bread you're eating, not the man's hand."[12]

When emphasizing the sanctity and significance of the church, Keeble used the following illustration:

> "E" on a gas gauge means empty. Once I looked over and saw the tank was empty, and right down at the foot of the hill was a gas station. It was night, and there was a sign that said, "Open 24 hours a day." This station owner said he had white gas, ethel gas and regular gas. He recommended the ethel gas because it would take the knocks out of the car. That's what we ought to do in the church of Christ—stay open for business day and night, and we ought to use the "ethel gas" because it takes the knocks out—the knocks out of life.[13]

In 1930, Keeble's parabolic preaching proved successful in establishing what is now the Woodlawn Forrest Church of Christ in Valdosta, Georgia. He told his audience a story about his wife, Minnie, who thought she had paid off a furniture debt. The White bookkeeper, however, told her that she still owed one more payment. Mrs. Keeble returned home, frustrated and confused, but afterwards, she found the receipt that stated, "Paid in Full." She then thanked God, returned to the store, and showed the clerk the receipt. Keeble appropriated the story to drive home a spiritual message: "Above everything keep your receipts. If you are going to heaven and you appear before Jesus Christ at the final consummation of all things and at the judgment seat of Christ where all nations must appear and you stand there and you haven't got a written receipt by Jesus Christ, signed with His blood, you will have to check off with your debt unpaid."[14]

The preaching of Marshall Keeble, then, was both belligerent and practical. Michael Casey has rightly noted that Keeble's sermons differed from other Black preachers such as G. P. Bowser (1874–1950) and R. N. Hogan (1902–97), who often quoted large portions of Bible passages. Conversely, Keeble's deliveries tended to be parabolic. "Keeble used a specific technique in his storytelling and analogies," asserts Casey, "that Hogan apparently did not use: his stories or 'parables' were filled with double meanings."[15] In one way, Keeble stressed a biblical message that his listeners needed a receipt from the Lord—namely, baptism for the remission of sins to enter heaven. Such a homily would have appeased his White supporters in his faith tradition. In another way, Keeble emphasized "keep your receipts" to subtly remind African Americans in his audience that not having documentation could lead to continuous indebtedness to White merchants.

A Preaching Strategy

But Keeble also had a preaching strategy. Each year, Keeble implemented a seven-point plan of action that led to his unparalleled successes. First, at the start of the New Year, Keeble conducted a lengthy gospel meeting for his home congregation, the Jackson Street Church of Christ in Nashville. Second, during the winter months, Keeble often received several calls from White leaders in Churches of Christ, arranging for him to evangelize their African American neighbors. After closing a successful gospel campaign with fifty-five baptisms and twelve restorations in Tyler, Texas, in the fall of 1935, Keeble reported, "The white church here called us to labor here. Brother Harvey Scott labors here. He did all in his power to make the meeting a success."[16]

Third, Keeble, after having received monetary and material support from A. M. Burton and other White benefactors, arrived in a particular city and customarily stayed with a Black family. Fourth, if no African American Church of Christ family lived in the local community, the renowned evangelist found housing with a respectable Black "sectarian" family. Fifth, Keeble preached to racially segregated listeners and baptized Black candidates, but

White seekers often (in conformity to Jim Crow statutes) received baptism at the hands of White church leaders. When Keeble, African American seekers, and Anglo supporters assembled for an evangelistic meeting, they unabashedly paid homage to both the God of heaven and to a "god of segregation." One student of Keeble's extraordinary life has observed,

> White Christians admired and eagerly sought Keeble's talents, gladly welcoming him into their communities to evangelize African Americans, and attending the gatherings themselves. But at the same time they refused to host him in their own homes or allow him to preach in their own church buildings as Jim Crow principles held firm in Jackson [Mississippi] and throughout the South.[17]

Sixth, Keeble's powerful and parabolic preaching led to a Black congregation being planted in a Southern town. He then added the newly planted church to the subscription list of the *Gospel Advocate*. The White contributors to the journal profoundly shaped the theology of those new Black Churches of Christ. Keeble himself once confessed that it does "my soul good when I read the *Gospel Advocate*." Seventh, Keeble returned the following year or sent one of his many ministerial proteges to help stabilize the fledgling congregation.[18] These seven steps, with minor exceptions, constituted the Keeble strategy, which drew and maintained a rigid line between White and Black saints in Churches of Christ.

Notwithstanding his system of evangelistic outreach, Marshall Keeble often found himself subjected to physical abuse and racial violence. Some Black denominationalists, upset with his exclusivist pronouncements, threatened to "tar and feather" him and burn down his tent. On one occasion, while preaching in west Tennessee, a White man came to the front of the audience during the invitation and "struck" the Black evangelist a "staggering blow on the left side of his head with brass knuckles." Keeble was stunned for the moment but regained his composure, got up, recovered, and "turned the other cheek." The White assailant, Howard Sanford, then fled away into the woods, but later died of alcohol poisoning a year later. His tragic demise caused many witnesses of the physical assault to think that God had taken vengeance on Sanford.[19]

Throughout his preaching career from 1914 to his death in 1968, Keeble encountered many verbal threats and faced multiple physical attacks. Yet he remained true to his commitment to the advancement of the "pure gospel." His diligence and sacrifice left an indelible mark on the history of African American Churches of Christ particularly and Churches of Christ in general.

NOTES

[1]Annie C. Tuggle, *Another World Wonder* (n.p., 1973), 112.

[2]Keeble, "Among the Colored Folks," *Gospel Advocate* 59 (Oct. 11, 1917): 996. See also Robinson, *Show Us How You Do It*, 21.

[3]For Keeble, the phrase "pure gospel" meant evangelizing through the local congregation without missionary societies, worshiping with no instruments of music, baptizing adult believers for the remission of sins, and organizing churches with elders and deacons.

[4]Keeble, "Among the Colored Folks," *Gospel Advocate* 63 (Aug. 4, 1921): 748.

[5]E. N. Glenn, "Keeble in California," *Christian Leader* 47 (May 16, 1933): 7; Robinson, *Show Us How You Do It*, 2.

[6]Choate, *Roll Jordan Roll: A Biography of Marshall Keeble* (Gospel Advocate, 1968), 2, 18.

[7]Keeble, "News and Notes," *Gospel Advocate* 75 (Feb. 2, 1933): 119; S. H. Hall, "The Death of Sister Keeble," *Gospel Advocate* 75 (May 4, 1933): 429. See also Robinson, *A Godsend to His People: The Essential Writings and Speeches of Marshall Keeble* (University of Tennessee Press, 2008), xiv.

[8]Gene C. Finley, ed., *Our Garden of Song: A Book of Biography of Song Writers of the Church of Christ and Articles and Other Items of Interest of Our Worship in Song* (Howard, 1980), 174–76.

[9]Arthur Lee Smith Jr., "A Rhetorical Analysis of the Speaking of Marshall Keeble" (MA thesis, Pepperdine University, 1965), 4. Smith studied under Marshall Keeble at the Nashville Christian Institute and later changed his name to Molefi Kete Asante.

[10]Matthew C. Morrison, "Marshall Keeble's Eloquence of Disarming Humor," *Today's Speech* 17 (Nov. 1969): 17.

[11]Forrest Neil Rhoads, "A Study of the Sources of Marshall Keeble's Effectiveness as a Preacher" (PhD dissertation, Southern Illinois University, 1970), 201.

[12]Willie T. Cato, *His Hand and His Heart: The Wit and Wisdom of Marshall Keeble* (J. C. Choate Publications, 1990), 14.

[13]Cato, *His Hand and His Heart*, 50.

[14]B. C. Goodpasture, ed., *Biography and Sermons of Marshall Keeble, Evangelist* (Gospel Advocate, 1952 [1931]), 25–26. For more parables of Keeble, see Edward J. Robinson, *Hard-Fighting Soldiers: A History of African American Churches of Christ* (University of Tennessee Press, 2019), 57–71.

[15]Michael W. Casey, *Saddlebags, City Streets, and Cyberspace: A History of Preaching in the Churches of Christ* (Abilene Christian University Press, 1995), 148–51. See also Robinson, *Show Us How You Do It*, 68.

[16]Keeble, "From the Wide Harvest Field," *Firm Foundation* 52 (Oct. 1, 1935): 6.

[17]Robinson, *Show Us How You Do It*, 113.

[18]Robinson, *Show Us How You Do It*, 69.

[19]Robinson, *Show Us How You Do It*, 211.

CHAPTER SIX

THE LATER YEARS

Edward J. Robinson

Marshall Keeble (d. 1968) lived through times of momentous change for his people. World War II led to many pivotal social shifts in the United States. The response of the United States to the bombing of Pearl Harbor (which took place on Keeble's sixty-third birthday) and its entry into the global conflict helped lift the nation out of the Great Depression. During the war, one million Black Southerners left their homeland in search of economic and social opportunities in the North and in the West. In 1944, the *Smith v. Allwright* decision of the US Supreme Court declared the White primary unconstitutional.

Shortly after the Second World War, Harry Truman (1884–1972), a Democrat from Missouri, championed the cause of civil rights. John Hope Franklin and Evelyn Brooks Higginbotham have pointed out, "Just as Truman had proclaimed it America's duty to lead and defend the free world internationally, so he charted a similar course at home. Speaking from the Lincoln Memorial in June 1947, he declared, 'We must make the Federal Government a friendly, vigilant defender of the rights and equalities of all Americans. . . . Our National Government must show the way.'"[1] The next year, President Truman desegregated the armed forces. These events clearly illustrate the far-reaching changes in American policies that would restructure and reshape Keeble's world.

The political and social rumblings of the 1940s foreshadowed a decade of social and racial upheaval in the South in the 1950s. The *Brown v. Board of Education* decision of 1954, the brutal execution of Emmett Till (1955), the Montgomery Bus Boycott (1955–56), and the Little Rock Nine episode (1957) exposed the virulent racism that engulfed the lives of Black Southerners. To combat anti-Black perspectives and practices swirling across the United States, African Americans established nonviolent organizations such as the Southern Christian Leadership Conference (SCLC) and the Congress of Racial Equality (CORE) to work for equal rights, while rigidly and rabidly racist White Southerners formed their own reactionary groups, such as the White Citizens Council and a revived Ku Klux Klan, which were, along with Strom Thurmond's earlier Dixiecrat political initiative and the 1960s revival of the Republican party in the South, designed to thwart federal intervention in civil rights.[2]

Keeble seldom if ever commented on these events publicly, although he was certainly aware of them. In fact, he delivered several speeches on lectureship programs at Church of Christ-related schools in the South that excluded Black students. Even after Keeble became president of the Nashville Christian Institute, White Christian colleges (connected to Churches of Christ) continued to close their doors to Black students. In 1950, Keeble spoke at a lectureship at Abilene Christian College in Texas, where he heaped praise on White administrators at the newly established Southwestern Christian College, who trained "boys and girls of the Negro race . . . to get out and meet anybody that rises up against the church of Christ." Knowing that most Church of Christ colleges rejected African American students, he concluded his speech with a mild rebuke: "May the grace of God dwell in your heart and may the grace of God cause you to look upon no race as being inferior, but let's make him what he ought to be and lift him on a higher plane that Jesus can bless you and give you a crown that fadeth not away."[3]

Purity in the Pulpit

Notwithstanding the extraordinary changes sweeping across the nation, Keeble kept carefully to his chosen evangelistic work while working to shape the morality and ethics of Black congregations. Many of his articles in the 1950s focused on "purity in the pulpit," jealousy among church leaders and members in Black Churches of Christ, as well as congregational division and disputes and virtuous living. Keeble's passionate love for members of the Church of Christ prompted him to chide Black congregants. "It seems like the more our brethren learn from the word of God," he wrote, "the more we try to show how smart we are. . . . If we keep on fighting on the inside of the church we should remember that we are committing suicide spiritually."[4] Because he planted so many congregations with his preaching, he felt obligated to help bring them to spiritual maturity, thereby adding to his own duties.

But why would Marshall Keeble emphasize moral purity in preachers' lives? The tragic death of Paul D. English (1910–40) might offer a clue. A native of Dickerson, Tennessee, English relocated to Nashville and received baptism at the Jackson Street Church of Christ, Keeble's home congregation. After the death of his father, English relocated to Chicago, Illinois, with his mother, but later returned to Tennessee to matriculate at what is now Tennessee State University in Nashville. English married Novella Cannon of Tullahoma, Tennessee, and the couple had four children. In 1940, Paul and his wife relocated to New York City, where there was no Black Church of Christ. But within a week, Paul English had planted a Church of Christ for African Americans in Harlem.[5] In the summer of 1940, Mrs. English shot and killed her husband, Paul. Did Brother English have an extramarital affair that precipitated his death? Or did Sister English act out of a fit of rage? The details of the murder are nebulous. An African American newspaper reported, "Charged with homicide, Mrs. Novella English told police she had wrested the gun from her husband a few moments before the shooting."[6] As this horrendous event became known, Black leaders and members in Churches of Christ were deeply troubled and saddened. Annie C. Tuggle described Paul English as a young man with "brilliant wit and talent." Having intimate knowledge of English and his family from the Jackson Street congregation in Nashville, Marshall Keeble was no doubt heartbroken and disturbed as to why this tragedy occurred. It was perhaps this episode, among others, that prompted the esteemed evangelist to issue calls for moral purity and holy living among African American preachers and members in Churches of Christ.

In the 1950s, Keeble consistently sounded the alarm urging preachers to pursue holy and righteous living. "I am worried over the many traps that are being set for our preaching brethren," warned Keeble, "and I am afraid that some will walk into these traps if caught and not watching." He then added, "If Satan overthrew Adam, Noah, Lot, and Moses, he will overthrow us and cause us to fall and disgrace the church if we are not careful. Satan is going about as a roaring lion seeking whom he may devour (1 Pet. 5:8), and we must buffet our bodies and bring them under subjection lest after we have preached to others we be a castaway (1 Cor. 9:26, 27)."[7]

Keeble further admonished fellow Black preachers to avoid flirting with women and to resist other moral temptations. He wrote:

> Here are some of the danger signs of a preacher weakening. When we begin to be successful and people begin to praise us, most of us are not able to stand it. We begin to dress in a way that makes us appeal to some weak sisters and they soon discover that we are trying to entice them. Now my advice to all preachers is to not try to dress so attractively, because in dressing in this way you make the wrong impression on both the brothers and sisters and cause them to lose confidence in you and your sermons will lose their power. When a preacher loses control of himself and begins to let weak sisters entice him, he not only loses power and influence but finally he will have to stop preaching because no one appreciates his sermons.[8]

Keeble continued to express caution over Black preachers who used their position as an evangelist to "flirt" with women. He stressed:

> Preachers are allowed in our homes at any time because the brethren have confidence in them. But when a preacher takes advantage of his confidence and betrays trust and begins to flirt with the women, he begins the most dangerous thing he could allow himself to do, because it will surely destroy him. There are some women who just stay set for weak preachers and they are so perfect they know a weak preacher the first time they lay eyes on him.

"I am sorry we have weak preachers among us," lamented Keeble, "and weak sisters who delight in ditching or to overthrowing a weak preacher. Brethren, I hope this article will cause our preaching brethren to resist these temptations."[9]

Marshall Keeble's foregoing words attest that the premier Black evangelist in Churches of Christ was not concerned only about doctrinal orthodoxy, but he was also preoccupied with moral and sexual purity. The preacher's comments also reveal that, by the 1950s, Keeble had expanded his ministerial roles, working as a church planter, educator, evangelist, missionary, and moral counselor.

Church Growing Pains

The ethical teachings of the apostle Paul greatly shaped Keeble's moral pronouncements. Taking his cue from the apostle's catalog of vices delineated in Galatians 5:19–20, Keeble affirmed:

> A real Christian would not be caught at a card party, because it is a form of gambling and has caused thousands to stumble. At most parties, beer, whiskey, and wine are served; and if you refuse to play cards and drink these strong drinks at these parties, they will make fun of you; and sometimes the pressure is so heavy we yield, and then we cause someone to stumble, and the church of Christ is hindered in its work of saving souls and lifting Christ up.

"It is impossible to lift Christ up," he lamented, "while drinking beer, whisky, wine, and dancing at these worldly parties. They destroy our souls."[10]

In an article titled "Weights and Sin," Keeble warned his readers against the harm of spiritual weights. "When we are loaded down with weights we are likely to sink into sin and be eternally lost." He then specified the spiritual weights: "smoking, card playing, theatergoing, dipping snuff, petting, drinking wine and strong drinks. Many other things I could mention."[11]

More than a pious pontificator, Keeble endeavored to practice what he preached. "Card playing is found in many Christian homes," he fussed. When preaching in Huntsville, Alabama, he recalled being invited to go home with a group of card players. "After I got there," he remembered, "I found that they wanted to know if they obeyed the gospel could they continue to play cards. I told them to obey the gospel and they wouldn't desire to play cards anymore and all of them were baptized." Expressing a desire to be a good example before Black believers, Keeble added, "Had I played cards with them they may have refused the gospel. It is best to never let weights cause people to be lost. We are all so careless about causing people to stumble."[12]

As a moral counselor who traveled extensively in and out of Black congregations, Keeble sensed growing power struggles between preachers and elders in African American Churches of Christ. In an article titled "Preachers and Elders," he rebuked African American preachers who appointed only elders who totally agreed with their decisions, writing, "Some elders agree with everything the preacher says or plans, so the preacher can praise them. A preacher who takes advantage of elders this way is the one that is not qualified and not the elders the preacher has attacked, and made them cowards by threatening to move them." Keeble chided Black preachers who used their authority to intimidate elders. "And when such a preacher gets all of the elders afraid of him," he added, "he takes over the whole church and becomes the only one qualified to take the oversight. He then becomes the boss and ruler and he thinks the church cannot dismiss him because he has all of the elders afraid, men who have served as elders for years before he came along." In Keeble's view, an overbearing evangelist "crushed" the elders and forced them to resign or stop working "as elders because they are made to believe that the preacher must lead."[13]

In Keeble's mind, African Americans in Churches of Christ also experienced growing pains, which manifested in conflict between church leaders as well as struggles between the flesh and the Spirit. In an article called "The Works of the Flesh and the Fruit of the Spirit," Keeble highlighted adultery in Paul's catalogs of vices in 1 Corinthians 6:9–10 and Galatians 5:19–20. "Adultery is mentioned first and this is causing many children of God to fall," wrote Keeble. "I am sorry to have to say that many preachers are guilty of adultery, and I am offering this suggestion to my preaching brethren. Don't try to look so attractive in the pulpit, because there are a good many weak women in the church and they begin to admire the preacher."[14]

Knowing the pervasive influence of the preacher, Keeble elaborated:

> Now here is my brotherly advice to all preachers. Dress neatly and clean but never allow yourself to become a fashion plate. If you do you hold yourself up and not our Lord. Another very dangerous thing is trying to use big words. It often causes people to not appreciate our message. And another dangerous thing is preachers allowing an envious spirit to enter their hearts. If your fellow preacher can preach better than you, don't envy him, but learn to praise one another. The Scriptures teach that we should give honor to whom honor is due and praise to whom praise is due. I hope all of us will remove all envy, malice, and jealousy from our hearts, because these are works of the flesh and they cause us

> to lose our influence and effectiveness as we strive to bring people to Christ.[15]

Elder Statesman

Keeble viewed himself as a true team player. He never displayed in his words and deeds any jealousy or harbored any animosity against fellow Black preachers in Churches of Christ. He cast his full support behind G. P. Bowser (1874–1950) and his educational enterprise at the Bowser Christian Institute in Fort Smith, Arkansas, and his paper, the *Christian Echo*. Writing in 1945, Keeble lavished praise on Bowser. "You are now doing your greatest work," boasted Keeble. "I hope you will live to see your plans fully developed; because you have never become discouraged, and your faithful wife [Fanny Bowser] has stood by you through these many years of hardships and trials. You have been a blessing to the church ever since I saw you obey the Gospel."[16] Here Keeble perhaps was referencing Bowser's 1904 confession of faith at the Jackson Street Church of Christ in Nashville.

Keeble affectionately added more of Bowser: "You have been a blessing to me; and anytime I can be of any assistance, please call on me." He went on to applaud the work of H. H. Gray, R. N. Hogan (1902–97), Levi Kennedy (1899–1970), G. E. Steward (1906–79), and J. S. Winston (1906–2002). Keeble called these men "great workers in the Kingdom of God. With such men standing with you [Bowser], there is nothing but success." Keeble, while preaching in Atlanta, Georgia, in 1945, then mentioned his own work at the Nashville Christian Institute, noting, "I have two of our little boy preachers with me, and all that hear them are greatly impressed." The little preacher boys would have been Robert Woods, Fred Gray, Hassen Reed, and/or Robert McBride.[17]

In the 1950s and 1960s, Keeble was more than a spiritual encourager and moral counselor. The liberality of White Christians that had enabled him to traverse the United States now allowed him to travel abroad as a global missionary, touring and preaching in Africa, Asia, and Europe. After his foreign sojourns, Keeble recorded and published an account of his travels in *From Mule Back to Super Jet with the Gospel*. This work and the articles he wrote for the *Gospel Advocate* took no account of the tumultuous political and social episodes of the 1960s; the assassinations of John F. Kennedy, Malcolm X, Martin Luther King Jr., and Robert F. Kennedy were never referenced in his essays. If Keeble showed no public interest in these momentous events, he was definitely touched by the deaths of his lifelong White supporters and comrades: Nicholas B. Hardeman (1965) and A. M. Burton (1966). Perhaps more devastating to Keeble personally than the demise of those pivotal figures was the closure of "his school," the Nashville Christian Institute, in 1967.[18] Paradoxically, while the death of Jim Crow opened doors of opportunity for Black students, it also quickened the collapse of NCI as schools once closed to African Americans across the South now opened to them.

After the closure of NCI, Black and White leaders in Churches of Christ fought in court over assets worth half a million dollars, and Keeble supported the White establishment in Nashville and opposed many of his Black former students. The demise of NCI and its subsequent legal skirmishing left Keeble brokenhearted and fractured the fellowship between Anglo and African American believers, leaving wounds that still linger.[19]

Conclusion

What then was Marshall Keeble's legacy in his later years? Keeble's role in his later years was multifaceted. On the one hand, he continued to plant congregations across the American South, although they were fewer. Such evangelistic success undoubtedly thrilled his soul. He also rejoiced when fellow Black preachers such as G. P. Bowser and R. N. Hogan garnered success. On the other hand, growth of African American Churches of Christ created growing pains as preachers and elders engaged in struggles for power. Many of his articles in the 1950s focused on moral rectitude. In the 1960s, during the fervor of the Civil Rights Movement, Keeble, funded by many of his generous White supporters, traveled abroad and preached in Africa and Europe. The closure of NCI in 1967 also pained him, causing him to lament, "While Sister Keeble and I regret to see Nashville Christian Institute close her doors, we wholly support what we thought had to be done. We live in a new day. We must be a part of that new day, there is no other way."[20] The death of Jim Crow birthed new opportunities for Black youths in Churches of Christ to attend public schools across the South. Saddened to see the old days of NCI fade, Keeble relished the thought that his spiritual grandchildren now stood in the brightness of a new day with better opportunities.

NOTES

[1]John Hope Franklin and Evelyn Brooks Higginbotham, *From Slavery to Freedom: A History of African Americans*, 9th ed. (McGraw-Hill, 2011), 500–501.

[2]For an overview of key events in the African American struggle for civil rights, see Franklin and Higginbotham, *From Slavery to Freedom*.

[3]Keeble, "The Church among the Colored," in *Abilene Christian College Bible Lectures* (Firm Foundation, 1950), 156.

[4]Keeble, "Among the Colored Brethren," *Gospel Advocate* 93 (June 21, 1951): 399.

[5]This biographical information was composed from Annie C. Tuggle, *Our Ministers and Song Leaders of the Church of Christ* (Annie C. Tuggle, 1945), 56.

[6]"Wife Held for Death of Harlem Evangelist," *The Afro American* (Aug. 10, 1940): 8.

[7]Keeble, "Among the Colored Brethren," *Gospel Advocate* 93 (May 17, 1951): 317–18. This article is titled "Purity in the Pulpit." See Robinson, *A Godsend to His People*, 47–48.

[8]Robinson, *A Godsend to His People*, 47–48.

[9] Robinson, *A Godsend to His People*, 47–48.

[10] Keeble, "Among the Colored Brethren," *Gospel Advocate* 93 (Feb. 1, 1951): 78–79.

[11] Keeble, "Among the Colored Brethren," *Gospel Advocate* 93 (Apr. 26, 1951): 269.

[12] Keeble, "Among the Colored Brethren," *Gospel Advocate* 93 (Apr. 26, 1951): 269.

[13] Keeble, "Among the Colored Brethren," *Gospel Advocate* 93 (Apr. 12, 1951): 238.

[14] Keeble, "Among the Colored Brethren," *Gospel Advocate* 93 (July 26, 1951): 478–79.

[15] Keeble, "Among the Colored Brethren," *Gospel Advocate* 93 (July 26, 1951): 478–79.

[16] Keeble, "Encouragement Letter," *Christian Echo* 40, no. 10 (June 20, 1945): 3. For a biographical sketch of Fannie Bowser (1869–1947), see R. Vernon Boyd, *Undying Dedication: The Story of G. P. Bowser* (Gospel Advocate, 1985), 20, 99.

[17] Keeble, "Encouragement Letter." See also Robinson, *A Godsend to His People*, 36; Robinson, *Show Us How You Do It*, 115.

[18] Richard T. Hughes, *Reviving the Ancient Faith: The Story of Churches of Christ* (Eerdmans, 1996), 292–95.

[19] Keeble, "Nashville Christian Institute to Close," *Gospel Advocate* 109 (Mar. 16, 1967): 166. See also Gary Holloway and John York, eds., *Unfinished Reconciliation: Justice, Racism, and Churches of Christ* (Abilene Christian University Press, 2003).

[20] Keeble, "Nashville Christian Institute to Close," 166. See the full text of this article in Appendix Two.

CHAPTER SEVEN

EVANGELISM AND THE CONSTANT CHALLENGE OF RACE

Tanya Smith Brice

Marshall Keeble was born in Murfreesboro, Tennessee, on December 7, 1878, a little more than a decade after the end of the US Civil War. Whites and former slavers were strategizing about the fate of freedmen in this new context. One Tennessee newspaper published an article titled "African Colonization" that posited:

> . . . there are many cogent reasons why the immediate colonization of Africa, by the colored people of the South, should be encouraged by all good friends of both races. 1. Neither can be so prosperous and happy as both would be, if separate and living in different countries. . . . 2. The execution of this plan will not only remove an incubus from the white race, but it will also

> increase the commercial activity of the nation, while it can be made a source of profit to individual citizens. . . . 3. Colonization in Africa offers to the negro [*sic*] himself the only prospect, which he can possibly find, of realizing his hopes for social advancement or political preferment. . . . Socially or politically he will find there no barrier in his way to eminence.[1]

This is one example of many that suggests there was little desire for Tennessee Whites to live alongside the formerly enslaved as equal citizens.

In addition, Keeble was born during the yellow fever epidemic of 1878. One newspaper reported, "Owing to the yellow fever Fisk University at Nashville, Tenn., has but one-third as many pupils as usual this season. One fatal case of the disease has occurred. President Cravath, of the University, has returned from Europe with the Jubilee Singers, who have disbanded. Prof. H. S. Bennett has also returned after spending three months abroad."[2] The newspapers in towns throughout Tennessee were fraught with accounts and death tolls of those who were afflicted with yellow fever. The freedmen were less likely to die from yellow fever than Whites, resulting in an increase in Black citizens, particularly in Memphis.[3] As the number of freedmen increased and the number of Whites decreased, racial tensions erupted, resulting in the rise of domestic terrorism toward Black citizens.[4]

The era of Reconstruction had just ended in 1877. Blacks in Tennessee were exerting their civil rights as freedmen. Domestic terrorist groups, such as the Ku Klux Klan, led by Grand Wizard Nathan Bedford Forrest of Memphis, terrorized Black Tennesseans to discourage political participation, land ownership, and education. Chattel slavery was replaced with a new system of slavery, convict leasing, resulting in an increase of Blacks in the state penal system. Despite these efforts, Black Tennesseans, in partnership with Northern abolitionist missionaries, founded Fisk University and Central Tennessee College (currently known as Walden University) in 1865, Roger Williams University (currently known as American Baptist College) in 1867, LeMoyne Institute (now LeMoyne-Owen College) in 1869, Knoxville College in 1875, and, Meharry Medical College in 1876. Lane College was founded in 1878 or 1882 by the Christian Methodist Episcopal Church, making it the only Black institution of higher education founded solely by Black Tennesseans. It was in this context that Keeble was reared and with this lens that he engaged in his ministry of evangelism.

Churches of Christ were first listed in the 1906 Federal Census of Religion as a subset of the "Disciples or Christians" denomination. According to this census, there were 2,649 congregations established by 1906.[5] Most of these congregations were found in the South Central part of the United States (primarily Kentucky, Tennessee, Arkansas, Oklahoma, and Texas) and in the North Central part of the United States (primarily Indiana, Missouri, and Kansas). Interestingly, there were only four "colored" parsonages reported as Disciples of Christ and/or Churches of Christ in this census.

The Spiritual Formation of Keeble

In 1895, Marshall Keeble was baptized at the Gay Street Christian Church in Nashville by Preston Taylor (1849–1931), an influential African American businessman and minister. Keeble's ministerial and evangelistic style was influenced by evangelist Samuel W. Womack (1851–1920). According to the 1900 US Census, the Womack family boarded with the Keeble family in Davidson County, Tennessee. Keeble married Womack's daughter, Minnie, in 1896. Womack saw his conversion to this movement as a liberating transition "from the old world of slavery to the new world of freedom."[6] Womack was impressed by the seemingly positive treatment that he received by White congregants. He recounted, "We were allowed to meet and worship with them for a number of years. In partaking of the Lord's Supper we were all waited on just alike. The wine and bread were not brought to us at the same time it is brought to us in some of the churches that I meet with for worship now."[7]

Undoubtedly, Womack passed this optimism about White Christians to Keeble as he began his storied career in planting African American congregations of Churches of Christ. However, Womack was not blind to the racialized attitudes among Christians. He wrote:

> It does seem to me that something ought to be said and done to change the moral and religious attitudes of the two races toward each other. Only a few of the whites have much or any confidence in the black man, and so many have none; and the blacks seem to stand that way toward the whites. I am proud to say, however, that it is not that way with the writer. When I begin with the year 1865 and think of such [White] men as Dr. Brents, Lee, Trimble, T. J. Shaw, Darnell, Dixon, Bolding, Barrett, Fanning, the Sewells, the Lipscombs, and many others, who, in holding their meetings would ask for room and seats for the colored people, and, after preaching, would come around and shake our hands, I am made to feel very grateful.[8]

By 1902, Womack and Keeble transitioned from the Disciples of Christ to the Churches of Christ, as evidenced by their fund-raising for and planting of the Jackson Street Church of Christ in Nashville. Keeble became so proficient at church planting that he has been described as "almost like some divine magician [because he] seemed to speak black congregations into existence."[9]

Evangelizing in the Midst of Racism

In spite of the American apartheid system of Jim Crow laws, Keeble established approximately three hundred African American congregations of Churches of Christ, and he baptized upwards of forty thousand people throughout the United States, primarily in the South. As noted earlier, Keeble identified seven influences to his evangelistic success: "a supportive spouse, skillful tutelage, personal zeal, white philanthropy, a mild disposition, constant prayer, and homiletical skill."[10]

Paradoxically, White philanthropists who financed Keeble's ministry were motivated not only by evangelistic concerns but also by social ones. They saw Keeble's work as a tool to maintain racial segregation among congregations and, likely most important, as instruments of social control and social alienation. After an evangelistic campaign led by Keeble in Valdosta, Georgia, that resulted in 329 baptisms of both Blacks and Whites, Alexander Bigby Lipscomb (1876–1940), the nephew of David Lipscomb, observed:

> The work among the colored people here was sponsored and financed by the white disciples. We have never made a better investment for the Lord nor any which brought such quick and happy results. Such preaching has not only created a new religious and moral status for the Negro element, but it has brought to this community a new citizenry capable of thinking in terms of the Bible. This means that we now have better farm hands, better porters, better cooks, better housemaids than ever before.[11]

Lipscomb's sentiments were normative among White Christians and provided a rationale for the continued philanthropic support of Keeble's evangelistic efforts. Lipscomb went on to justify this continued support: "Is it not fitting that the descendants of the race whom our fathers kept in the bondage of human slavery but to whom civilization brought the gift of emancipation, should now be led by the white children of the present generation out of the darkness and bondage of sin into 'glorious liberty of the children of God'?"[12]

While these racist sentiments were widespread across the Church of Christ fellowship,[13] there were some White Christians who pushed back against such anti-Black attitudes. John Moody McCaleb (1861–1953), a missionary to Japan, wrote:

> The Negro has intellect. I speak of him in particular because he is supposed to be the lowest of the races. It is often said that the mental and moral character of the negro is altogether inferior to that of the white man; that he is intellectually a fool; that he is lazy, dishonest, untruthful, and unfeeling. My opinion is that there are as many good people, naturally, among the negroes as among the rest of mankind. . . . there is no natural difference between them and other people. . . . God has made of one all the nations to dwell upon the face of the earth. The fact that Jesus died for all shows that all are of one nature and one blood.[14]

White Christians struggled with the influence of the domestic terrorism groups on their congregations during this time period. In a letter to the *Gospel Advocate*, a reader asked the following question: "I am asking you for information. Can a man be a member of the 'Invisible Empire' (the Ku Klux Klan) and at the same time be a follower of Christ? I have my doubts that it is possible." H. Leo Boles (1874–1946), editor of the *Gospel Advocate*, responded:

> I know but little about the Ku Klux Klan; but from what I do know about it, I would say that no Christian ought to be a member of it. No one can follow Christ and go into this, neither did he give any instruction for any of his people to go into it. Therefore, no one can claim Scriptural authority for being a member of it. The Ku Klux Klan has been outlawed in many sections of the country. I am sure that it does not make one a better Christian to belong to it. Like all other social organizations, what good it may have can be enjoyed by the child of God as a Christian in the church of Christ; therefore, one need not go into it for any spiritual blessings or for any instruction as for living the Christian life. Much harm has grown out of the Ku Klux Klan. It has been a menace to our civilization and should not be encouraged even by citizens of our government, to say nothing of Christians, who should keep themselves unspotted from the world. I can think of no reason that could be assigned for any Christian's going into the Ku Klux Klan. . . . I know of Gospel preachers who were led into the Klan, but they have seen the error of their way and turned from it. I hope that all of the Lord's people may see the error of being in the Klan and have the courage to come out of it and serve in the name of Christ their fellow men and honor and glorify God in his church.[15]

Marshall Keeble relied heavily upon the financial support of Whites, including some who unapologetically expressed anti-Black, racist ideologies. Keeble maintained a docile, humble attitude in the presence of these philanthropists, which guaranteed their continued financial support. Foy E. Wallace Jr. (1896–1979), a Church of Christ minister and editor of the *Gospel Advocate*, wrote of his disdain for racially integrated gospel meetings, interracial cooperation between Christians, and "social equality" between Whites and Blacks. Wallace (1941) wrote:

> Reliable reports have come to me of white women, members of the church, becoming so animated over a certain colored preacher as to go up to him after a sermon and shake hands with him *holding his hand in both of theirs*. That kind of thing will turn the head of most white preachers, and sometimes affect their conduct, and anybody ought to know that it will make fools out of the negroes. For any woman in the church to so far forget her dignity, and lower herself so, just because a negro has learned enough about the gospel to preach it to his race, is pitiable indeed. Her husband should take her in charge unless he has gone crazy, too. In that case somebody ought to take both of them in charge.[16]

In this same article, Wallace lamented about an African American couple who directed an orphanage and who he believed "favor[ed] social equality" because of their close work with "white brethren [who were] apparently encouraging them." Wallace went on to express strong disapproval of the following situation:

> The young editor of "Christian Soldier," in the valley, admits that he roomed with the negro preacher, R. N. Hogan, and slept in the same bed with him two nights! And he seemed to be proud of it! Aside from being an infringement on the Jim Crow law, it is a violation of Christianity itself, and of all common decency. Such conduct forfeits the respect of right-thinking people, and

> would be calculated to stir up demonstrations in most any community if it should become generally known.

Recognizing the influence that Keeble had on the African American church and its ministers, Wallace wrote:

> I have always said that Marshall Keeble and Luke Miller [Keeble's contemporary] could not be spoiled, but if I ever hear of them doing anything akin to such as this, I will take back every good thing I have ever said of them. Keeble should teach these negro preachers better than that, even if we cannot teach some young upstart among the white preachers. Their practices will degrade the negroes themselves. It is abominable.

In his humble fashion, Keeble responded to Wallace:

> Dear Sir and Brother in Christ:
>
> For over thirty years I have tried to conduct my work just as your article in the *Bible Banner* of March suggested. Taking advice from such friends as you have been for years has been a blessing to my work.
>
> So I take the privilege to thank you for that instructive and encouraging article. I hope I can conduct myself in my last days so that you and none of my friends will have to take back nothing they have said complimentary about my work or regret it.
>
> Please continue to encourage me in my work and *pray for me*.
>
> Fraternally yours, M. Keeble[17]

This exchange demonstrates Keeble's pragmatism when interacting with Whites who both supported his evangelistic efforts and were hardened racists. While Keeble traveled broadly throughout the United States, he was subjected to the racist mores of the time. He was hosted by Black families and establishments because of segregation laws. He was subjected to physical and verbal abuse from Whites as he traveled. Yet Keeble continued to place himself in humiliating and dangerous situations because he truly believed in the work in which he was engaged. Willie Cato (1923–91), White minister, travel companion, and leader of African Christian Schools, reported Keeble as saying, "I have had to rely upon God, he is the only one I had. The white man didn't like me because of the color of my skin. The colored man didn't like me because of my religion. Now, son, who else did I have?"[18]

Keeble undoubtedly felt as if he did not have a comfortable space in his ministry. Whites were suspicious of him because he was Black. Blacks were suspicious of him because of the denomination that he promoted, Churches of Christ. There were seven historically Black denominations in existence during Keeble's life: African Methodist Episcopal Church (1816), African Methodist Episcopal Zion Church (1821), Christian Methodist Episcopal Church (1870), National Baptist Convention (1880), Church of God in Christ (1897), National Baptist Convention of America (1915), and the Progressive National Baptist Convention (1961). These denominations were founded in response to racist ideologies among White Christians; Keeble, in contrast, promoted an openly racist denomination. In such a situation, Keeble believed that he could only rely on God's love and comfort.

Defying Expectations

The Greek poet Dinos Christianopolous wrote, "They tried to bury us, but they didn't know we were seeds." This saying exemplifies the life of Marshall Keeble. He lived an extraordinary life that defied expectations. Keeble was born in rural Tennessee to formerly enslaved parents. He had a seventh-grade formal education. He was able to exegete the Bible in a way that influenced thousands to obey the gospel of Jesus Christ. He influenced the planting of hundreds of congregations of Churches of Christ.

Keeble skillfully engaged in this work with the philanthropic support of Whites who supported him to preach a gospel that on the surface supported the maintenance of a racist, segregated society. Although Keeble was invited to communities to preach the gospel, he was often subjected to racist attacks and humiliations while there.

As president of Nashville Christian Institute, a preparatory school for African American children from elementary to high school from 1942 to its closing in 1967, Keeble influenced hundreds of teachers and preachers. Some of the most notable alumni include Fred Gray, civil rights attorney; Dr. W. F. Washington, long-time minister of Golden Heights Church of Christ, Fort Lauderdale, Florida; Dr. Molefi Kete Asante, father of the academic study of African-centered thought; the late Dr. Jack Evans, longtime president of Southwestern Christian College; Daniel Harrison, director of the National Crusade for Christ; and the late R. C. Wells, director of the National Lectureship.

Keeble presented as a docile, meek, humble, almost subservient preacher before White philanthropists, which is known as the "magical negro trope."[19] That is, Keeble interacted among Whites in a nonthreatening way to ensure that Whites were comfortable around him. Consequently, he is fondly remembered among Whites as a model Black preacher. Keeble had several contemporaries who were also holding gospel meetings, baptizing African Americans, and planting African American congregations, such as Samuel Robert Cassius (1853–1931), G. P. Bowser (1874–1950), and Alexander Cleveland Campell (1866–1930), but those names are not widely known among Whites.[20] On the other hand, Keeble believed in the concept of racial self-help, as is evidenced by his "fruit" among African American leaders and congregations across this nation. "While he did not openly espouse an end to segregation, Keeble's stoicism in the face of white intimidation and violence revealed his faith, determination, and discipline, traits that also characterized later civil rights activists who practiced nonviolent direct action."[21]

Keeble's pragmatism left an indelible mark on Churches of Christ. He was indefatigable in his pursuit of the building of the Lord's church and the saving of souls. While Keeble's pragmatism enabled him to endure unspeakable insults and abuse, his "fruit" has sprung forth to challenge racial injustices in and out of the Churches of Christ while continuing the work of kingdom building.

NOTES

[1]"African Colonization," *Clarksville Weekly Chronicle*, Jan. 4, 1873, *Chronicling America: Historic American Newspapers*, Library of Congress, https://chroniclingamerica.loc.gov/lccn/sn88061082/1873-01-04/ed-1/seq-1/.

[2]*The Milan Exchange*, Oct. 17, 1878, *Chronicling America: Historic American Newspapers*, Library of Congress, https://chroniclingamerica.loc.gov/lccn/sn86053488/1878-10-17/ed-1/seq-2/.

[3]L. E. Blake and M. A. Garcia-Blanco, "Human Genetic Variation and Yellow Fever Mortality during 19th Century U.S. Epidemics," *mBio* 5, no. 3 (July 1, 2014), doi:10.1128/mBio.01253-14; J. H. Ellis, "Disease and the Destiny of a City: The 1878 Yellow Fever Epidemic in Memphis," *West Tennessee Historical Society Papers* (1974): 27.

[4]C. Carney, "The Contested Image of Nathan Bedford Forrest," *Journal of Southern History* 67 (2001): 601–30, https://doi.org/10.2307/3070019.

[5]United States Bureau of the Census, Censuses of Religious Bodies, 1906, https://www2.census.gov/prod2/decennial/documents/00190438p1ch1.pdf.

[6]Robinson, "'The Two Old Heroes': Samuel W. Womack, Alexander Campbell and the Origins of Black Churches of Christ in the United States," *Discipliana* 65 (Spring 2005): 3–20.

[7]Womack, "Attitude of the Races," *Gospel Advocate* 59 (Dec. 30, 1915): 1326–27.

[8]Womack, "Attitude of the Races," 1326–27.

[9]Robinson, *Show Us How You Do It*, 1.

[10]Robinson, *Show Us How You Do It*, 2. This list is a summary by White leader E. N. Glenn who heard Keeble explain his success as an evangelist. The article is titled "Keeble in California," *Christian Leader* 47 (May 16, 1933): 7.

[11]A. B. Lipscomb, "It's Not Keeble, but the Bible Is Right," *Christian Leader* 45 (Aug. 25, 1931): 6.

[12]Lipscomb, "It's Not Keeble, but the Bible Is Right," 6.

[13]Tanya Smith Brice, *Reconciliation Reconsidered: Advancing the National Conversation on Race in Churches of Christ* (Abilene Christian University Press, 2016); Crawford, *Shattering the Illusion*.

[14]J. M. McCaleb, "The Negro," *Gospel Advocate* 46 (Mar. 17, 1904): 166.

[15]H. Leo Boles, "Query Department," *Gospel Advocate* 69 (Mar. 10, 1927): 232.

[16]Foy E. Wallace, "Negro Meetings for White People," *Bible Banner* (Mar. 1941): 7—emphasis in original.

[17]Keeble, "From M. Keeble," *Bible Banner* (Apr. 1941): 5.

[18]Willie Cato, "Keeble as a Teacher," *Gospel Advocate* 110 (July 18, 1968): 452. See the story told by Cato and his daughter in Appendix One.

[19]David Ikard, *Lovable Racists, Magical Negroes, and White Messiahs* (University of Chicago Press, 2017); Robinson, *The Magic Negro in Churches of Christ: Marshall Keeble's Unique Relationship with White Churches of Christ* (audio recording, Sept. 18, 2007, https://texashistory.unt.edu/ark:/67531/metapth792334/ accessed June 2, 2024), University of North Texas Libraries, The Portal to Texas History, crediting Abilene Christian University Library.

[20]Robinson, *To Save My Race from Abuse: The Life of Samuel Robert Cassius* (University of Alabama Press, 2007); Barclay Key, *Race and Restoration: Churches of Christ and the Black Freedom Struggle* (Louisiana State University Press, 2020); R. Vernon Boyd, *The Story of G. P. Bowser: Undying Dedication* (Gospel Advocate, 2001).

[21]Key, *Race and Restoration*, 51.

PART THREE

MARSHALL KEEBLE

His Legacy

CHAPTER EIGHT

BUILDING ON THE LEGACY

Jefferson R. Caruthers Jr.

Marshall Keeble was a product of his times. As full and distinctive as was his life and ministry, varying factors converged in history to produce the man, his work, and his influence. This reality takes nothing away from the unique gifts and talents that characterized his life but rather provides a broader and more informative explanation of why things occurred as they did—as well as why his impact is felt to this day.

Keeble was descended from enslaved parents in his home state of Tennessee, which was one of the Southern states that fought vigorously, even to the death, for what they often referred to as "our way of life." That way of life, benefiting from productive agrarian enterprises and chattel enslavement, became the common cause—and eventually a "lost cause"—for states below the Mason–Dixon Line. Rebel states fought for this cause until surrender to the North was their only means of survival. Defeated rebels surrendered many things, not the least of which was a way of life that by law enabled them to sell, purchase, enslave, hunt, capture, and re-enslave men and women.

Social Separation and Christian Unity

After the war, enslavers and emancipated persons found themselves occupying the same geographical space but reckoning with vastly different realities. And these realities, for White leaders and colored converts within the Stone–Campbell Movement, included how to justify expected social separation while emphasizing unity among those confessing faith in Jesus Christ as Savior.

African Americans were represented in all three divisions of the Stone–Campbell Movement,[1] a movement that emphasized unity among believers, informed by a belief that if they could unite on what the scriptures alone taught, then they could recapture the church in its purest form, creating unity among all believers.[2] African Americans eventually became most numerous in Churches of Christ.[3]

In the South, Churches of Christ became the dominant group of representatives of the Stone–Campbell Movement. Their ultimate distinction from others within this tradition included a reluctance to support missionary societies, an insistence on worshiping with a cappella music, separation from other faith groups, and a hermeneutical approach that emphasized pattern, blueprint, direct command, approved example, and necessary inference, as well as discovering biblical truths through inductive reasoning.[4] A key part of their approach to the Bible, and consistent with the religious environment of the nineteenth century, was the strong conviction that the common man and woman had as much ability to understand the Bible on his or her own as did any cleric or educated Christian leader.

Anglo American members of Churches of Christ in the South found themselves faced with the reality that those who were once enslaved were now freedmen. They were part of a shared Christian heritage of restoration principles. How were Whites to interact, engage, and fellowship with their sable brothers and sisters? What responsibilities, in their own minds, did they have to these fellow believers?

Restoration leaders like David Lipscomb and Tolbert Fanning answered like Southerners throughout the South. They realized that freedmen were still a part of everyday society. Their labor was still needed. They occupied the cities and towns. And they continued to worship. But working with a consciousness of desired unity, while at the same time faced with a growing separation of the races, a working arrangement needed to be found that allowed both unity and separation. This unity would manifest itself primarily in aid to support the planting and growth of African American churches, while also keeping the races separate at a time when society was digging its trenches to fight against the mixing of the races.

Colored Preachers Worthy of Support

Partnerships of support for African American preachers who would take the gospel to the world of the freedmen was part of the thinking of Anglo Americans well before A. M. Burton and others became main contributors to the ministry of Marshall Keeble.

Early on, written and preserved for posterity, there was an anticipated "want ad" circulated in the *Gospel Advocate*. The job description, character traits, and rationale for support of freedmen were already detailed in the early months after the war. Anglo Americans would support a man of humble and gentle character, one of industry, one who would not "lift up his heels" against those in the Anglo American community, one who could be accepted by both Blacks and Whites.

Focused on these basic requirements, editors of the *Gospel Advocate* detailed expected attitudes of freedmen who would qualify for support. For example, as long as the Negro was "unassuming," Lipscomb thought it was wise to support him. He wrote of the colored brother, George Ricks, who was in Alabama: "We have the assurance from Brother Chisolm and others that Brother Geo. Ricks is a most worthy, unassuming brother, and is doing a good and faithful work for the Lord and his people."[5] Of another colored brother, he wrote, "This is from our colored brother A. N C. Williams of Franklin, Tenn. He is their teacher and is a modest, unassuming, industrious Christian gentleman, seemingly anxious to learn his duty and to do it."[6]

Lipscomb spoke well of George Ricks and A. N. C. Williams, brothers who were industrious, modest, and unassuming. These brothers would be worthy of support from the White brothers. But there were others who were characterized as persons who "lifted up their heels" against their White brothers. Tolbert Fanning, Lipscomb's co-editor, noted:

> For more than thirty years we took very great interest in the religious education of the colored race; but at the inauguration of the late war, from causes which we need not state, most of our sable brethren became alienated from our people and forsook our counsel. This we deeply regretted, but they hearkened to the voice of strangers, and, generally, became the enemies of their former associates and friends. Men that had aided in purchasing their freedom, and partially educated, lifted up their heels against us.[7]

Freedmen who did not display proper respect and deference toward Whites should not expect to receive support. On another occasion, Tolbert Fanning observed:

> We have several colored brethren in this section, whose scholarship and general intelligence would enable them to be useful in the cause of education and religion, but, in their present state of mind we doubt the propriety of the experiment. They are slow to act in harmony with their intelligence and religious advantages surpassing those of their race in any other section in our knowledge, and the greatly excited political condition into which they have been recently thrown, it seems to us, wholly disqualifies them for teaching the religion of Jesus Christ. Should future developments, however, have the tendency to produce a change in our views of a more favorable character, it will afford us great satisfaction to cooperate with them in the amelioration of their race.[8]

Both Lipscomb and Fanning believed that it was the mission of Whites to support work among the coloreds. They would become responsible for creating a description of the character freedmen needed to display to receive support. The supported preacher must be unassuming, industrious, modest, and not one who would lift up their heels against their former enslavers.

In the early twentieth century, Marshall Keeble, more than others, met these qualifications. Keeble not only met the qualifications, he exceeded the most hopeful expectations of his supporters. He owned not just a partnership with Anglo Americans but also a certain calling from God to preach to his people, to call them to receive salvation in Christ, to promote an adherence to a Bible deemed "always right," defending the faith and championing the cause of nonsectarian Christianity. He could allay the fears of White supporters, appease Southern Whites, and provide leadership to colored brothers and sisters who would become members of Churches of Christ. These abilities led others to acknowledge a genius to his thought and behavior. His work and influence would remain strong throughout the greater part of the twentieth century.

The Legacy

Marshall Keeble's legacy included an evangelistic and missionary focus, seeking to preach to men and women everywhere. He wanted African American converts to continue their growth. He sought to make provision for their studies through Bible class materials, and he trained preachers. He worked to develop preachers who could effectively preach and teach the gospel, as well as develop local churches. He was committed to Christian education. He appreciated the value of print communication as a tool for informing and unifying the brethren. He championed the faith by a willingness to debate the truth of Bible teachings. But undergirding all of this was an exceptional genius that allowed him to secure the financial and social support needed to travel and navigate his way through a mostly Southern ministry by partnering with Anglo Americans. It was a partnership that would often meet the criteria of friendship and brotherhood, even though it worked eventually to create a separate fellowship. Not many preachers of these times could work under the conditions Marshall Keeble did.

The South had already dismissed the lofty goals of Reconstruction when Keeble entered ministry. The challenges of segregation (de jure and de facto), and growing civil rights activity all informed the world in which he lived. During these times, the people he ministered to were once "freedmen," then "coloreds," properly "negroes" (though often pronounced "negras" by White Southerners). In the 1950s and 1960s, his converts were "Black" and proud, "Afro-Americans," "African Americans," and, for a few, simply "Americans." They were uneducated and educated, economically poor, on the fringes of society, and a very few, well-to-do. Religiously, they were both holy rollers and partygoers; responsible for their families, and irresponsible; surrounded by family and left by family members migrating to perceived better opportunities in other regions of the country. These were the settings and realities that Marshall Keeble faced as he proclaimed God's gospel truths. He was effective in every circumstance. His successes informed and made solid his legacy.

Building on the Legacy

Generations that followed built on the legacy of Marshall Keeble by a commitment to evangelism that took the gospel to all the world. One witnesses this continued legacy, beyond Keeble's lifetime, as Churches of Christ maintained a calendar that included what was usually called the "gospel meeting." These meetings had the specific aim of presenting the gospel to persons outside of fellowship with God, not having obeyed the truth and been baptized for the remission of sins. Messages not only lifted up Jesus as Savior, but there was heavy emphasis on the "true church" and scriptural practices of worship. These meetings often continued for two weeks or more. Extended meetings of this nature continued into the 1990s, with the main focus on making new converts.

Closely aligned to tent meeting efforts expecting mass conversions was an effort known as the Crusade for Christ. It was organized by Daniel Harrison and by preachers, leaders, and churches in the Chicago area. The first crusade was held in Chicago in 1979. These campaigns recruited church members throughout the brotherhood who would converge on a designated city for the purpose of knocking on doors, setting up Bible studies, gathering for daily teaching sessions, and ending with nightly preaching. After the first year, Dr. Jack Evans, a student of Marshall Keeble and Nashville Christian Institute, was the featured speaker for over three decades.

Educating preachers is another facet of Marshall Keeble's legacy. During Keeble's lifetime, young people traveled from across the country to attend school at Nashville Christian Institute. Another institution, Southwestern Christian College, founded by G. P. Bowser in 1948, also focused on training preachers. Jack Evans served as president of SWCC from 1967 to 2016. Ministerial students from SWCC have filled a great number of pulpits of African American churches. Also within the tradition of educating preachers, the School of Religious Studies was founded by Lloyd Harris in Greenville, Mississippi, in 1978.

The legacy of unifying churches greatly impacted the identity of African American churches. Through the means of periodicals, lectureships, songs, and worship practices, members of African American churches enjoyed a consistent experience of worship and practice from city to city, state to state, and region to region. The *Christian Echo* was the main periodical source for African American churches throughout the twentieth century. Founded by G. P. Bowser in 1902, the paper was an independent source of communication to African American church members. In 1989, another paper that gained wide circulation among Blacks was Herman Wesley's *Revivalist*.

Marshall Keeble supported brotherhood lectureships as a means of fostering unity among African American church members. Beyond the years of Keeble, continuing in the legacy of lectureships, African American church members established regional and state lectureships that adopted purposes consistent with the National Lectureship founded in 1945. These included the Southeastern Regional Lectureship in 1974, the Midwest Lectureship in 1976, the Gulf Coast Lectureship in 1976, and the

Northeast Lectureship in 1983. Among African American women, a ladies' lectureship was formed in 1985. All of these benefit from a legacy of work in establishing churches in the South through its most influential preacher, Marshall Keeble.

Keeble was a man of his times, shaped and molded for the work God called him to do. For all times, his legacy will impact Churches of Christ and the Stone–Campbell Movement. The hope is that his work of unity in a context of separation will eventually strengthen a unity that can one day negate separation.

NOTES

[1]Early historians of the Disciples of Christ note that "Negroes were included in the membership of the Cane Ridge, Kentucky, and Brush Run, Pennsylvania, churches as well as in others of the earliest congregations of the Disciples." See Winfred Ernest Garrison and Alfred T. DeGroot, *The Disciples of Christ: A History* (Christian Board of Publication, 1954), 468. In Christian Church history, Earl Ervin West noted that Peter Lowery, a formerly enslaved brother, had led efforts to evangelize among African Americans for nearly two decades. See West, *Search for the Ancient Order: A History of the Restoration Movement, 1919–1950* (Religious Book Service, 1987), 4:238.

[2]For an examination of the thought of returning to a "first times" existence that informed, among other church fellowships, leaders in the Stone–Campbell Movement, see Richard T. Hughes and C. Leonard Allen, *Illusions of Innocence: Protestant Primitivism in America, 1630–1875* (University of Chicago Press, 1988).

[3]From the late nineteenth century into the twentieth century, African American Churches of Christ were able to grow at a greater rate than were those associated with the Disciples of Christ and Christian Churches. Leroy Garrett noted, "Unlike the other churches in the Movement, the Churches of Christ have a substantial brotherhood of black churches, with a long and impressive history, 'tolerated but not wanted,' to quote [Floyd] Rose, separate but not equal." Leroy Garrett, *The Stone-Campbell Movement: An Anecdotal History of Three Churches* (College Press, 1981), 680.

[4]Eugene Boring underscores the influence of J. D. Thomas as a proponent of these hermeneutical principles among Churches of Christ in the mid-twentieth century. He notes that Thomas was influenced by David R. Dungan, *Hermeneutics: A Text Book*, 2nd ed. (Standard Publishing, 1888) in M. Eugene Boring, *Disciples and the Bible: A History of Disciples Biblical Interpretation in North America* (Chalice Press, 1997), 283–88. See J. D. Thomas's work, *We Be Brethren* (Biblical Research Press, 1958). Beginning in the 1960s, a group of scholars began moving beyond the traditional hermeneutic, so that by the 1990s, a significant stream of White Churches of Christ had moved away from the pattern approach toward a focus on conforming the church to the image of Christ. Two voices of this shift—one earlier and one later—are Thomas H. Olbricht, *Hearing God's Voice: My Life with Scripture in the Churches of Christ* (Abilene Christian University Press, 1996), and more recently, John Mark Hicks, *Searching for the Pattern: My Journey in Interpreting the Bible* (Amazon Digital Services, 2019).

[5]David Lipscomb, "Letter from a Colored Brother—Help Wanted," *Gospel Advocate* 10 (Jan. 2, 1868): 24.

[6]Lipscomb, "The Cause among the Colored People in Franklin, Tenn.," *Gospel Advocate* 21 (Aug. 21, 1879): 537.

[7]Tolbert Fanning, "Three Days in Convention with the Freedmen," *Gospel Advocate* 9 (June 6, 1867): 447.

[8]Fanning, "Colored Mission," *Gospel Advocate* 9 (Aug. 31, 1867): 610.

CHAPTER NINE

"IN HIS OWN WAY"

Fred D. Gray and the Legacy of Keeble

Edward J. Robinson

The 1940s proved to be an extraordinarily challenging decade. On December 7, 1941, the attack by the Japanese on Pearl Harbor pulled the United States into World War II. Several months later, President Franklin D. Roosevelt (1882–1945) signed Executive Order 9066, which consigned seventy-five thousand Japanese citizens on the West Coast to relocation camps during World War II. The commitment of the federal government to winning the war opened up jobs for American Blacks in northern and western communities and simultaneously precipitated high levels of Black migration. In the summer of 1943, a race riot erupted in Detroit, Michigan, where twenty-five African Americans and nine Whites were killed and where several hundred thousand dollars in property was demolished.[1]

In this racially charged milieu, African American leaders had an epiphany: They came to understand that it was useless for Black soldiers to fight against fascism in Europe while Black citizens found themselves subjected to racial discrimination and racial violence at home. As two historians have poignantly observed, "During World War II, black Americans unapologetically battled on two fronts, committed to a 'Double-V' campaign—for victory over the racism in America and for victory over the fascism that American troops fought to destroy on foreign soil."[2] Notwithstanding the pervasive racism swirling across the United States, African Americans demonstrated their patriotism by signing up to fight in World War II. Approximately one million Black men and women served in segregated units.[3] In his 1944 book, *What the Negro Wants*, Rayford W. Logan (1897–1982) collaborated with other Black intellectuals (Mary McCloud Bethune, Sterling Brown, W. E. B. Du Bois, Langston Hughes, A. Philip Randolph, Roy Wilkins, and others) who emphatically called for an end of segregation and racial discrimination and demanded "first class citizenship" for African Americans.[4]

While the aforementioned dramatic events stirred the racial pot in American society, Marshall Keeble (1878–1968), the newly appointed president of the Nashville Christian Institute, was busy traversing the country to promote the cause of Christian education for Black youths. Established in 1940 in Nashville, Tennessee, by White philanthropists and Black leaders in Churches of Christ, NCI was a preparatory school for African American youths serving grades K–12 (until its closure in 1967).

Among the "Boy Preachers"

Fred D. Gray, a thirteen-year-old African American from Montgomery, Alabama, came under Keeble's influence at the school and accompanied him on fundraising tours over a four-year period,

Keeble with preacher boys from Nashville Christian Institute.
Back row, from left: Hasson Reed, Robert McBride
Front row, from left: Robert Woods, Marshall Keeble, Fred Gray

1943–47. In his inspiring and informative speech at the Keeble symposium (September 20–21, 2023) at Lipscomb University in Nashville, Tennessee, Gray delineated his connection with Keeble while matriculating at NCI.[5] In his speech, he acknowledged, "My direct contact with Bro. Keeble was a relatively short period of time. During the time I was a student at the Nashville Christian Institute (NCI) from 1943–47, he was president of the school."[6]

Before coming under the guidance of Marshall Keeble, Gray had come under the tutelage of Sutton Johnson. A native of Middle Tennessee who received baptism at the hands of Keeble at age fourteen, Johnson began preaching the following year while studying at the Silver Point Christian Institute, a school organized by G. P. Bowser (1874–1950) to educate Black young people in Churches of Christ. He served the Simpson Street Church of Christ in Atlanta, Georgia, and planted a Black congregation in Macon before making his way to Montgomery, Alabama, where he served the Holt Street Church of Christ from 1942 to 1945. Researcher Pearl Gray Daniels, a sister of Fred Gray, has noted, "During Brother Sutton Johnson's tenure as Minister of the Holt Street Church of Christ, he taught and encouraged young boys to become ministers. He helped them to develop sermons and allowed them to practice speaking before the church." "He urged the parents," Daniels observed, "to send their sons to Nashville Christian Institute."[7]

One of the young men from that congregation who matriculated at NCI was Fred Gray. His father had died when he was two years old.[8] Thus, when Gray arrived on the NCI campus, Marshall Keeble became a surrogate spiritual father. Gray recalled, "A year after I became a student, Bro. Keeble became president. He properly did not qualify to be a teacher under Tennessee law."[9] Keeble had limited academic training, having never surpassed the seventh grade.[10] But notwithstanding his limited knowledge, Keeble understood the culture of the South, and he fully understood his responsibility as president to be twofold: to raise money for NCI and to recruit students.

To accomplish this task, Keeble allowed "two boy-preachers" to accompany him and to "speak before he would preach." Gray explained that Keeble "would raise a collection and ask the audience to send their boys to NCI, even if you have problems with them. He would say, 'If you send your boys to the school we will send them back men.'"[11] This is what Keeble did for Gray, Robert Woods, Richard Cooper, Freeman Wyche, Franklin Florence, David Jones, Ralph Moore, Hasson Reed, Robert McBride, and many others. They entered NCI as young boys and, under the tutelage and mentoring of Keeble, exited as young men.[12] Keeble not only blessed these young men, but Fred Gray established lifelong relationships with some of his NCI classmates.

Three Trips with Keeble

Gray referenced three trips that he and fellow students made with Keeble. The first excursion in 1943 took them from Nashville, Tennessee, to Albany and Valdosta, Georgia, to Jacksonville, Daytona, and Miami, Florida, and then up the west coast of Florida to Palm Beach, St. Petersburg, and Tampa, and then back to Nashville. On this trip, Gray and Richard Cooper, a student from Atlanta, Georgia, accompanied Keeble, and they succeeded in recruiting three future students: Freeman Wyche, Carol Taylor, and Franklin Florence, all of whom enrolled the following year.

On the second trip in 1944, Gray and Paul English traveled with Keeble to Memphis, Tennessee, and then to Arkansas, Oklahoma, Texas, Louisiana, and Alabama. It was on this trip that Gray and English swayed Ralph Moore and Hasson Reed to enroll at NCI. Gray testified that he "became sick on that trip and one of the sisters at the church in Oklahoma treated me."[13] Here,

Gray provides a glimpse into the system of segregation. In the 1950s and 1960s, Jim Crow statutes prohibited Blacks from being treated in White hospitals. Scholar Lerone Bennett Jr. has called segregation the "great wall," insisting, "The root rationalization for all this was sex." He then added, "Brick by brick, bill by bill, fear by fear, the wall grew taller and taller. The deaf, the dumb and the blind were separated by color. White nurses were forbidden to treat black males."[14]

Noted historian John Hope Franklin (1915–2009) has confirmed the veracity of Bennett's observation. Twelve years before Gray arrived at NCI, Juliette Derricotte, dean of women at Fisk University in Nashville, and three students traveled to Athens, Georgia, to visit family members. On the way, their car collided head-on with a White couple near Dalton, Georgia. Even though Derricotte and one of the students sustained serious injuries, they were denied admission and treatment at the local tax-supported hospital. Franklin, a Fisk University student from 1931 to 1935, recalled that Derricotte and the other seriously injured student received treatment in the office of a White doctor and then were "sent to the home of an African American woman who provided beds for sick or injured black patients. Sadly, the student passed away there during the night; and Miss Derricotte, after being transported to an all-Black hospital in Chattanooga, Tennessee, died the next night, November 7, 1931." Franklin remembered, "When the news of their deaths reached Nashville, the entire campus was plunged into a period of mourning and outrage that the university had lost a student and its young administrator to segregationist practices."[15]

On the third trip in 1945, Keeble took four students with him to Natchez, Mississippi, where they planted the Fourth Street Church of Christ. Gray's companions on this journey included Robert Woods (Gallatin, Tennessee), Robert McBride (Natchez,

Mississippi), and Hasson Reed (Atoka, Oklahoma). Paul Tucker (1914–2000), the White preacher for the local White congregation, was an earnest and concerned minister who invited Keeble to Natchez to preach to the African American community.

When traveling across the South, Keeble and his protégés often stayed in the homes of generous Black Christians. Segregation prohibited African Americans from lodging in many or most hotels and motels. When R. N. Hogan (1902–97) traveled 1,550 miles from Southern California to Houston, Texas, he "had to keep right on going, day and night, without stopping but for gas and oil, all the way through."[16] Martin Luther King Jr. (1929–68) spoke to these oppressive conditions Black people faced in his "I Have a Dream" speech, lamenting, "We can never be satisfied as long as our bodies, heavy with the fatigue of travel, cannot gain lodging in the motels of the highways and the hotels of the cities."[17] Thus, Keeble and his traveling students felt the sting of racial discrimination, and this burden went with Keeble over the many years of his incessant travel as an evangelist.[18] But the NCI president sidestepped the issue on these travels—as he did for the many years that followed. Gray testified, "There was nothing discussed during the trip about segregation nor race relations, nor anything about white people. Some of them attended some of the churches. Nothing about race was discussed with Bro. Keeble, all during the Civil Rights Movement."[19]

During the third trip, Tucker also arranged for Keeble to be photographed with his NCI students. This is a historic picture and appears in several textbooks, including on the cover of *Show Us How You Do It: Marshall Keeble and the Rise of Black Churches of Christ in the United States, 1914–1968*. Gray readily acknowledged that many young men who studied at NCI graduated to influential preaching posts, stating, "Of the early boy preachers only Freeman Wyche, who retired in Miami, and I are alive. Bro. Keeble took many other boy-preachers and leaders in their counties where they lived."[20]

"He's Too Smart!"

Marshall Keeble without question indelibly stamped Fred Gray's young life at NCI. After earning his high school diploma at NCI, Gray returned to Montgomery and studied at Alabama State University before earning his law degree at Case Western Reserve University in Cleveland, Ohio. Gray never forgot his roots and his indebtedness to Keeble and NCI. He consistently attended the annual lectureships at NCI, and when the board decided to close his alma mater, Gray spoke to Keeble in an attempt to prevent the demise of the school. Gray hoped that administrators at NCI would "give the Black Churches of Christ an opportunity to raise funds to keep it open, as they were doing with Southwestern Christian College in Terrell, Texas. I did not put any pressure on him. We simply filed a lawsuit against Lipscomb, AND THE REST IS HISTORY."[21] Gray and other Black litigants sought to get the almost half million dollars in assets transferred to the struggling Southwestern Christian College, but the Nashville court refused to grant the injunction against the White NCI board.[22] Ironically, the institution Fred Gray sued later bestowed on him an honorary doctorate (2014) and established the Fred D. Gray Institute for Law, Justice & Society on the Lipscomb campus in Nashville in 2016.

The teacher–student relationship between Marshall Keeble and Fred Gray was profound and paradoxical, and they shared striking similarities. First, both men were native Southerners and were blessed with longevity. Gray noted that his mentor "lived a long life from 1878 to 1968."[23] Gray himself has been blessed to live into his mid-nineties, where he has been afforded the opportunity to see the fruits of his labors, including the death of Jim Crow statutes as well as the rise of prominent African American leaders, including the first Black president of the United States (Barack Obama), the first Black vice president (Kamala Harris), and the first Black woman Supreme Court justice (Ketanji Brown Jackson).

Second, Keeble enjoyed a cordial relationship with the White establishment in Churches of Christ in Nashville and beyond because of his meek and mild posture on race relations. Gray, in contrast, adopted a bold stance against racial discrimination and the White establishment, but he has come to hold an esteemed place among White administrators at Lipscomb University and far beyond because of his accomplishments for racial justice. Before giving his speech at the "Keeble symposium" at Lipscomb University, Gray expressed gratitude for "Kimberly McCall, the Associate Dean of Academics and also Director of the Fred D. Gray Institute for Law, Justice & Society, for making all the arrangements for our visit."[24]

Third, Keeble firmly believed and preached that "baptism is for the remission of sins" and the Church of Christ was the one true church. When preaching in Valdosta, Georgia, in 1931, Keeble, in his sermon, "The Power of the Written Word," appealed to his Black listeners: "Now then, gentlemen, if your church is not on record, I wouldn't be in nothing—I am honest, friends, I am sincere, and I wouldn't be in nothing that couldn't be found on record. Be baptized and get into the church that we read about in God's written word."[25] Just as Keeble espoused a high ecclesiology, Gray over all these years has held a lofty view that members of the Church of Christ are on the right path to heaven.

Gray concluded his presentation at the Keeble symposium with the following observation: "Bro. Keeble was a wise religious man. He taught me so much more; most of which I have been using in my sixty-nine years as a civil rights lawyer, destroying segregation wherever I could find it." During his four-year stint at

NCI, Gray testified that "what I learned from [Keeble] has assisted me for all of my life up to the present."[26]

Gray also confessed, "I attended Bro. Keeble's funeral and would like to believe that he approved of what I did in the Civil Rights Movement. He would do that in his own way. . . . Finally, I think he would be well pleased with what Lipscomb University is doing as it relates to providing equal and fair education for all races."[27]

In conclusion, Marshall Keeble was adroit enough to evade the turbulent Civil Rights Movement, yet his refusal to "rock the boat" of race relations in the Jim Crow South profoundly and paradoxically prepared his pupil, Fred Gray, to overthrow that very system of segregation, which his mentor publicly ignored. Gray himself admitted, "You may say that Bro. Keeble played a major role in what I have done during the last sixty-nine years as a civil rights lawyer."[28]

When a preacher who had been at NCI later said to Keeble, "Fred Gray is smart. He is involved in the Civil Rights Movement," Keeble reportedly replied, "He's too smart!"[29] But Keeble was undoubtedly a secret admirer of and cheerleader for Fred Gray, along with Martin Luther King Jr. and others who contested the repressive system of segregation. Keeble openly complied with Jim Crow statutes, but he dared not let his White comrades know his true feelings and convictions. In the words of Black poet Paul Laurence Dunbar (1872–1906), Keeble "wore the mask." He without question supported Fred Gray secretly and cheered him on "in his own way." Keeble, in essence, was glad that his former NCI pupil was "too smart" and that he was strong enough to help derail the system of racial injustice designed to keep Blacks in a state of second-class citizenship.

NOTES

[1]John Hope Franklin and Evelyn Brooks Higginbotham, *From Slavery to Freedom: A History of African Americans*, 9th ed. (McGraw-Hill, 2011 [1947]), 469.

[2]Franklin and Higginbotham, *From Slavery to Freedom*, 451.

[3]Three years after World War II, President Harry Truman (1884–1972), a Democrat from Missouri, signed Executive Order 9981, which mandated the desegregation of the United States military. See Matthew F. Delmont, *Half American: The Epic Story of African Americans Fighting World War II at Home and Abroad* (Penguin, 2022), 287–88; Steven F. Lawson and Charles Payne, *Debating the Civil Rights Movement, 1945–1968* (Rowman and Littlefield, 1998), 7–8.

[4]Rayford W. Logan, *What the Negro Wants* (University of Notre Dame Press, 2001).

[5]Marshall Keeble ministered to and mentored many spiritual grandsons during his tenure at NCI. See Robinson, *Show Us How You Do It*.

[6]Fred Gray, "My Life with Marshall Keeble," Speech Notes, Carroll Ellis Symposium, September 21, 2023, Lipscomb University. For Gray's earlier account of his years at NCI, see his autobiography, *Bus Ride to Justice: Changing the System by the System—The Life and Works of Fred Gray*, rev. ed. (NewSouth, 2013), 7–9, 269–70.

[7]Pearl Gray Daniels, *The History of the Holt Street Church of Christ and Its Role in Establishing Churches of Christ among African Americans in Central Alabama, 1928–97* (American Literary Press, 1997), 48–49. Some of this biographical information was obtained from Annie C. Tuggle's useful work, *Our Ministers and Song Leaders of the Church of Christ* (Annie C. Tuggle, 1945), 82–83.

[8]Dan Abrams and Fred D. Gray, *Alabama v. King: Martin Luther King, Jr. and the Criminal Trial That Launched the Civil Rights Movement* (Hanover Square Press, 2022), 56.

[9]Gray, "My Life with Marshall Keeble," Speech Notes.

[10]Choate, *Roll Jordan Roll*, 17.

[11]Gray, "My Life with Marshall Keeble," Speech Notes.

[12]For an incomplete list of young men who attended NCI, see Robinson, *Show Us How You Do It*, 155–72, 183–84.

[13]Gray, "My Life with Marshall Keeble," Speech Notes.

[14]Lerone Bennett Jr., *Before the Mayflower: A History of Black America* (Penguin, 1988 [1961]), 256.

[15]John Hope Franklin, *Mirror to America: The Autobiography of John Hope Franklin* (Farrar, Straus & Giroux, 2005), 43–44.

[16]This story is told in Ira Y. Rice Jr., *Pressing Toward the Mark: An Autobiography* (G. T. Press, 1998), 157–65. See also Robinson, *The Fight Is On in Texas: A History of African American Churches of Christ in the Lone Star State, 1865–2000* (Abilene Christian University Press, 2008), 127.

[17]Martin Luther King Jr., "I Have a Dream," speech delivered on August 28, 1963, in Washington, DC. Transcript of the speech may be found at https://www.npr.org/2010/01/18/122701268/i-have-a-dream-speech-in-its-entirety.

[18] See the travel story told by Willie Cato, the White preacher who accompanied Keeble on his travels for many years—and the amazing conclusion to it told by Cato's daughter—in Appendix One.

[19] Gray, "My Life with Marshall Keeble," Speech Notes.

[20] Gray, "My Life with Marshall Keeble," Speech Notes.

[21] Gray, "My Life with Marshall Keeble," Speech Notes.

[22] Richard T. Hughes and James L. Gorman, *Reviving the Ancient Faith: The Story of Churches of Christ in America*, 3rd ed. (Eerdmans, 2024), 216.

[23] Gray, "My Life with Marshall Keeble," Speech Notes.

[24] Gray, "My Life with Marshall Keeble," Speech Notes.

[25] B. C. Goodpasture, ed., *Biography and Sermons of Marshall Keeble, Evangelist* (Gospel Advocate, 1952 [1931]), 27.

[26] Gray, "My Life with Marshall Keeble," Speech Notes.

[27] Gray, "My Life with Marshall Keeble," Speech Notes.

[28] Gray, "My Life with Marshall Keeble," Speech Notes.

[29] Gray, *Bus Ride to Justice*, 271.

CHAPTER TEN

A BRANCH OF THE TREE

W. F. Washington and the Legacy of Keeble

Orpheus J. Heyward

A significant fingerprint in the life of Marshall Keeble was his dedication to the training and development of preachers. Noted as a robust and influential evangelist, Marshall Keeble's ability to display the simplicity of the gospel became a noteworthy attribute of the preachers he developed. Under his preaching ministry, more than forty thousand were baptized and over three hundred congregations established in sixty years. The establishment of the Nashville Christian Institute, of which Marshall Keeble became president in 1942, is a centerpiece in Keeble's career and the heritage of African American Churches of Christ. From 1945 to 1955, 235 students graduated from this institution, and ninety-five became preachers.[1] Keeble believed the school was a training ground for young African American preachers who would carry on the gospel work in their communities.

Keeble recruited and mentored many students who later became influential leaders and ministers among African American Churches of Christ. Several of these influential leaders included the late Jack Evans Sr., president of Southwestern Christian College; W. F. Washington, minister of the New Golden Heights Church of Christ; and legendary civil rights attorney Fred Gray, who was recognized and honored by Lipscomb University in November 2023. Keeble's work at NCI was not only an educational endeavor but also a spiritual one. He saw his role as a mentor and a father figure to his students, whom he often called his "boys." These young men engaged in preaching, leading singing, and public recitation of Scripture that gained the attention of White audiences, resulting in their amazement and encouraging their support for the school. While much can be said about the closing of the school, which existed from 1941 to 1967, it was the catalyst for launching many effective and well-trained preachers who are extensions of the incredible legacy of Marshall Keeble.

An Extension of Marshall Keeble's Legacy in the Person of W. F. Washington

Among the prominent preachers who had a connection with Marshall Keeble, Dr. W. F. Washington is considered one of the leading voices within the African American Churches of Christ today. He was born and raised in Valdosta, Georgia. He was the great-great-grandson of an enslaved ancestor. As a youth, he traveled with other noted men in the fellowship of African American preachers. Some of these were Ulysses Shields, John Henry Clay (his father in the gospel), S. T. W. Gibbs Jr., and Alonzo Rose. He was also heavily influenced by R. N. Hogan and J. S. Winston, as well as a number of others.

At age eleven, Washington, known as "Willie" at the time, traveled from Valdosta, Georgia, to Nashville, Tennessee, to attend the

W. F. (Willie) Washington while he was a student at Nashville Christian Institute

Marshall Keeble with ten of his "preacher boys" (in the mid-1950s)

Nashville Christian Institute. He became one of Keeble's "boys." He traveled with Keeble and other ministers assisting in gospel meetings and promoting the institute. For example, in June 1953, under the tutelage of one of the preachers Keeble influenced, J. L. Cothron, "Willie" Washington participated in a gospel meeting in Vicksburg, Mississippi. Cothron complimented the young man, writing that he was "doing a good job singing and preaching." He continued, "Some say he is the best ever."[2]

As a powerful orator, debater, and church builder, the trajectory of W. F. Washington's ministry has significant parallels to that of Marshall Keeble. In particular, Washington became a noted gospel preacher who converted large numbers to Jesus. Many who have experienced his preaching were moved by his plainness, persuasiveness, and power, which reflect the preaching legacy of Keeble. Washington launched his congregational ministry in 1960 in Marshall, Texas, at the Westside Church of Christ while a college sophomore at Bishop College.[3] After serving for more than a decade there, he became the minister of the Golden Heights Church of Christ in Fort Lauderdale, Florida, in 1974, where he has served for fifty years and continues to do so.

During his time in Marshall, Texas, W. F. Washington graduated from Bishop College (a historic Black Baptist institution) and was subsequently hired by the president, M. K. Curry, as assistant dean of men. He also served as a part-time teacher and ultimately became dean of students. During his time at Bishop College, noted Baptist preachers who were tremendous orators often spoke in chapel. This exposure aided Washington in developing a unique style of preaching that cultivated an impressive oratorical ability while remaining deeply rooted in the faith professed among Churches of Christ.

After receiving his bachelor of science degree in social science at Bishop College, he pursued further academic study in criminal justice. He completed a master's degree in contemporary corrections at Sam Houston State University and a PhD in behavioral psychology at National Christian University.[4]

W. F. Washington is noted as a church builder, as evidenced by both of his local ministries in Marshall, Texas, and Fort Lauderdale, Florida. The Westside Church of Christ in Marshall began in 1929 under the leadership of G. P. Bowser. Washington began his ministry with the congregation when there were only twenty-five people present, and the congregation grew to two hundred while he was there.[5]

When he arrived in Fort Lauderdale in 1974, Golden Heights was a struggling church with 125 members, and by 1985, it was reportedly a thriving congregation of 2,700 members and 4,700 members by 1997, baptizing between 150–200 people every year.[6] The Golden Heights Church of Christ became known as one of the fastest-growing African American churches in Broward County and within African American Churches of Christ. On the fiftieth anniversary of the church in 1994 (and his twentieth anniversary as its minister), Washington credited the congregation rather than himself with the explosive growth due to their warm reception of people. Nevertheless, the growth was also due, in significant part, to the "respect that the church holds for Dr. Washington as a premier preacher in the Church of Christ nationally."[7] Importantly, however, a key part of his strategy for church growth and development was to engage in relevant community activity, the topic of the next section.

Ministry in the Community under the Leadership of W. F. Washington

"The black church," according to Washington, "is the mother of black history." It is the center of the Black community. "The church has paid its dues and stood the test of time," and it is the "one thing" African Americans can claim as their own. "That's all we have," he said. As reported, Washington believes that the primary goal of the Black church is "to offer spiritual guidance to a race of people confronted with the debris of slavery and discrimination—poverty, drug abuse and unemployment." The advances of the past decades in civil rights and social development would not have taken place "without the support of the black church and its leadership."[8] Consistent with this perspective, the Golden Heights Church of Christ, under Washington's leadership, has attempted to "effect change in the community through sixteen outreach ministries, including a school and crisis center." Moreover, this emphasis was part of Washington's first ministry with the Westside Church of Christ in Marshall, Texas. That church supported "a full-time hospital ministry, a jail house ministry, a full-time bus ministry, and a ghetto ministry," as well as supporting a mission point in Central America.[9]

On Education

W. F. Washington learned the value of education, at least in part, from Marshall Keeble. When he remembered that he was "born out of wedlock" and he was "reared by a grandmother and great-grandmother who were semi-illiterate,"[10] he was amazed by his blessings. He embraced the opportunities afforded him not only to complete a university terminal degree but to serve in educational institutions and promote education at all levels. While in Marshall, Texas, he taught at Pemberton High School and became its assistant principal as well as assistant track coach. Ultimately, he served his alma mater, Bishop College, in various capacities, as earlier noted. After he moved to Florida, he taught at the North Dade High School and was the assistant track coach there as well. Ultimately, his congregation in Florida established the Golden Heights Christian Academy in 1992.[11]

On Peace

In 1967, W. F. Washington felt compelled to write Martin Luther King Jr. after King announced his opposition to the Vietnam War. "I feel that you have been unduly criticized for your stand," wrote Washington. "As a minister you had to take a stand and as a fellow minister I was elated when you came forward." He praised King as one who worked for "peace for all mankind." (King had been awarded the Nobel Peace Prize in 1964.) As Robinson notes, "Washington then exhorted King to persevere amid the storm, 'keep the faith, and *this too shall pass*.'"[12] Washington maintained a high view of Dr. King and his work over time. In 2006, as he was interviewed about the meaning of the Passover, he said, "We use Exodus as a kind of storyline for our liberation," and he noted that King "was called a Moses of his people, who led them from Egypt through the wilderness. We allude to him as a deliverer, because black people made great strides under him."[13] Washington has served on the National Martin Luther King Jr. Memorial Committee.

In this spirit, Washington led a prayer vigil in Fort Lauderdale for the victims of the Atlanta child killings in 1981, where he stressed, "We'll even pray for the killer, whoever he is, that in some way he'll see the need to cease what he is doing. We will ask that he'll feel the pain he is inflicting on the city."[14] Washington advocated communal participation in prayer for peace and healing across all denominational barriers.

On Politics

During the 1988 election year, Washington invited politicians to speak at his church. "The church is open to all political candidates," he said. "I don't endorse anyone, but it's clear when politics are discussed which candidate I'm leaning toward." In addition, Washington committed "four buses at the church to make sure everyone can get to the polls," especially since he believed that the election "will determine what direction we go in the next few years." Nevertheless, Washington insisted that "there is a separation between politics and religion," although it is important to encourage people to vote—but "we don't tell them who to vote for."[15] After the election of Barack Obama in 2008, his congregation gathered to celebrate, and they shouted approval when he called Obama's election "a work of God." He rejoiced because Obama's election was testimony to the potential of every Black child, and he exhorted his congregation to get to work. "Get your kids off the street. Know your kids' teachers. Help them with their homework. Join the PTA. Obama can do his job, but we have to help." Reflecting this interest in participation, Washington has served on a national clergy committee. Nevertheless, when asked if he was a politician, he responded, "No, I'm saved and a Christian. That's sufficient."[16]

On Racism

Washington consistently praised civil rights leaders, including Martin Luther King, Nelson Mandela, and Jesse Jackson. When Jackson spoke in Fort Lauderdale in 1988, Washington called his speech "one of the most stupendous events in Afro-American history," excepting the contributions of Dr. King. Commenting on Nelson Mandela, Washington recognized that many might question some of his ideas about Christianity, "but when you take his work into context, he is the pre-eminent moral authority in the world today." That context was South African apartheid. In the context of his own African American experience, Washington was convinced that although "racism is like the weather; it will always be there," African Americans can "rise up and make a difference." He named three important factors: education, economics, empowerment. Washington contends, it was reported, "that the question of what racism has done to us should be inverted to the question, what have we done because of racism?"[17] Washington is a life member of the NAACP.

On Criminal Justice

Given Washington's academic training in criminal justice, it is not surprising that Golden Heights Church of Christ was addressing this problem as early as 1979. The church established a halfway house for young people exiting incarceration. As Washington reportedly said, the house does not work with "kids en masse" but "one at a time" for the sake of moral and spiritual development. "We think our approach will lead to better results for the society as a whole," he said. "If we can get just one or two of these kids to straighten out and make a contribution to society, then we've been a success."[18] Washington is a member of the American Criminal Justice Society.

An Interview with W. F. Washington

In preparation for this essay, I was honored to have the opportunity to interview W. F. Washington, during which time he provided insight into the nature and history of his ministry, including his time at Nashville Christian Institute with Marshall Keeble.[19]

On the Nashville Christian Institute

In response to a series of questions, Washington reflected on the importance of mentorship and what many influential preachers meant to his life, including Marshall Keeble. Ulysses Shields introduced him to the school when he was about eleven years old. His early interactions with Marshall Keeble's work were through an annual gospel meeting that he held in Valdosta, Georgia. Washington particularly noted a meeting in 1931 that resulted in 166 additions. The previous year saw the beginning of the African

American congregation in Valdosta, Georgia, with 159 additions as a result of Keeble's preaching and ministry, which is now the Woodlawn Forrest Church of Christ. The website of the church names "Willie F. Washington" as one who participated in the work of the congregation during the 1940s and 1950s.[20] During this era, Marshall Keeble would often come to Valdosta with young students, whom he would showcase to encourage support and allow the audience to see the fruit of the labor of the Nashville Christian Institute. These early experiences and the influence of Ulysses Shields led W. F. Washington to become a student at Nashville Christian Institute. Washington made clear that Marshall Keeble was heavily supported by the Caucasians (as was the beginning of the congregation in Valdosta) and shared a strong relationship with Athens Clay Pullias, who at the time was President of David Lipscomb College in Nashville.

The Nashville Christian Institute experience for W. F. Washington was not necessarily an introduction to the work of preaching. He already had experience with preaching, as he traveled with Ulysses Shields and John Henry Clay. In fact, he preached his first sermon at the age of nine before he went to NCI. According to Washington, most young men who attended the school received their initiation into preaching. However, he was fortunate enough to have had prior experience through previous mentors, and Marshall Keeble's impact was an added blessing to his journey in becoming an evangelist.

On Preaching

When asked about the strength of Marshall Keeble's preaching, W. F. Washington stated, "He was tremendously simple in his preaching and used parables." He was highly effective in a time when many African Americans did not have the opportunity of higher education. Accordingly, Washington believed Marshall

Keeble's preaching appealed to the masses; he was down to earth and easily received. Washington described his preaching with the word "illustrative." Additionally, Washington thought Keeble's preaching was challenging. He stated that Keeble would enter a city and challenge the denominational preachers. This was part of his apologetic style. He was confident in the truth of what Scripture presented, beckoning preachers to come down to the tent to prove him wrong.

As Washington provided a synopsis of Marshall Keeble's preaching, highlighting the simplicity yet profundity and his strong attack on denominational dogma, I asked him how this view of preaching impacted his understanding of the preaching task. He responded that it influenced him to the degree that it was a commitment and expectation to go into an area where the gospel had not been preached and establish a congregation through preaching that challenged false ideas of salvation. Following Keeble's example, he has established eleven congregations and participated in the establishment of numerous others. Today, it is often stated that W. F. Washington has baptized more people than any other living evangelist among African American Churches of Christ. This is an interesting parallel to the ministry of Keeble, who was renowned for the number he baptized.

On Religious Debate

Another aspect of training mentioned by W. F. Washington for African American preachers was engaging in religious debate. Within the fabric of the African American Churches of Christ, several fierce debaters were influenced by Marshall Keeble. According to Robinson, Luke Miller (1904–62), a spiritual son of Keeble and a prominent leader in the early years of the Valdosta congregation, was considered a highly skilled debater. Robinson mentions that Miller was much like his spiritual father in this regard, highlighting

Miller's debates with S. C. Johnson.[21] Like Keeble, Luke Miller had a tremendous impact on W. F. Washington, who continued the legacy of defending the faith through public debate.

In the interview, Washington mentioned Keeble's strategy when engaging in religious discussion. Keeble would say, "Dig a hole. Let them fall in it. Cover it up and stand on it." This methodology indicated that Keeble did not believe in chasing a person all over the Bible to explain every conceivable context. However, he would build an argument he knew the opponent could not disprove, consistently reminding the audience that the opponent had not yet answered the dilemma. Washington employed this methodology in his debate against a Seventh-day Adventist named Elder Baptiste. Washington worded the proposition in this way: "The Holy Bible teaches that the fourth commandment of Exodus 20 to keep the sabbath holy is commanded for New Testament Christians." He explained that his opponent would have to show the fourth commandment of Exodus 20 was commanded in the New Testament for Christians. He understood that no matter how hard his opponent would look, the fourth commandment of Exodus 20 is not in the New Testament, much less commanded to New Testament Christians. This was an example of how Dr. Washington would put in practice the Keeble maxim: "Dig a hole. Let them fall in it. Cover it up and stand on it."

On Mentorship

Knowing the impact of Marshall Keeble on so many preachers, I posed a question about the importance of mentorship, not just formal education. Honoring Keeble as an incredible gospel preacher, Washington spoke about recognizing those who have gone before us. He stated, "It is dangerous to destroy history." Deposits of the past play a significant role in the foundation upon which he stood. He greatly emphasized recognizing the pioneers who paved a path for us to travel. He viewed the work of these great pioneers as foundational and central to our identity. Washington has spent considerable time pouring into younger preachers in hopes that they would be strong in upholding apostolic truth. Many have become noted defenders of the faith, thoughtful expository preachers, and skillful church builders through his mentorship.

On Evangelistic Preaching

At the close of the interview, I solicited a final thought about the importance of evangelistic preaching. I asked, "It seems that training preachers in the defense of the gospel was considered a part of the preaching task. Would you agree that this was a significant part of the development of preachers in your day?" Washington responded, "Absolutely." Challenging doctrines antithetical to the gospel is part of the training and obligation of being a preacher. He reminisced about the process of going into a city with pamphlets and printed posters, flooding the community with literature concerning denominational churches. Poignant statements were made to demonstrate that the teaching of denominational churches opposed the Bible, the Word of God. As the topic continued to unfold, Washington admitted that it was not always stated positively and, at times, this approach drove people away since such statements were viewed as hostile and dogmatic. He alluded to the fact that some young preachers have decided to divorce themselves from the name "Churches of Christ" because of the past hostile activity. While Washington indicated that there were some instances when dogmatism had negative results, he also recognized that their commitment to the declaration of the gospel resulted in the expansion of God's kingdom.

Summation

Much can be learned from the life and legacy of W. F. Washington as a branch of the Keeble tree. His ministry reflects many parallel markers with that of his predecessor, Marshall Keeble. Both men had a passion for evangelism and church planting, a simplicity yet profundity in their preaching, and a strong defense of the gospel against denominational dogma. And Washington's example, following Keeble, shows the importance of mentorship, as he built upon the foundation of those who went before and who passed on their wisdom and experience to the next generation of preachers. Although Washington embraced some emphases absent from Keeble's public ministry, such as addressing questions of politics and race and focusing on located ministry, we can learn from his faithfulness, courage, and zeal as we seek to follow Christ and honor the spirit of the Restoration Movement.

On the website of the Golden Heights Church of Christ, Dr. Washington offers a word about his purpose in life, which summarizes the laudable faith of the pioneers and his own ministry: "to glorify God and His son Jesus Christ in the fulfillment of His mission on earth. To continue steadfastly in the Apostle's doctrine, fellowship, breaking of bread and in prayer. Confidently awaiting the glorious appearing of our Great God and Savior Jesus Christ."[22]

NOTES

[1]Don Haymes, "Nashville Christian Institute," in *Encyclopedia of the Stone-Campbell Movement*, Douglas Foster et al., eds. (Eerdmans, 2004), 552.

[2]J. L. Cothron, "News among the Colored Brethren," *Gospel Advocate* 95, no. 29 (July 16, 1953): 455.

[3]"Recognizing Current Preachers in the African American Church of Christ," Past and Present Preachers in the African American Church of Christ, accessed July 3, 2024, https://www.africanamericanchurchofchristministerslegacy.org/recognizing-contemporary-preachers-in-the-african-american-church-of-christ.html.

[4]His PhD dissertation was titled "Do Lower-Class Blacks Commit Suicide at a Higher Rate than Whites in a Homicidal Mode through Victim Precipitation Due to the Socialization Process and Role of Engulfment?" The research was an extension of the research by world-renowned criminologist Marvin Wolfgang of the University of Pittsburgh.

[5]"West Side Church Reported Growing," *Marshall News Messenger* (Jan. 30, 1972): 76.

[6]James D. Davis, "Passover Parallels," *Fort Lauderdale News*, Apr. 19, 1986, 51; Christian Walker, "Houses of Worship of All Denominations Abound in Tiny Lauderdale Lakes," *South Florida Sun Sentinel*, Sept. 1, 1997, 7; "W. F. Washington, Sr., PhD," Christian Living Books, https://christianlivingbooks.com/w-f-washington/.

[7]R. N. Hogan, "Thousands Attend Golden Anniversary," *Christian Echo* 84 (May–June, 1994): 5.

[8]Ricci Graham, "Black Churches Give More Than Religion," *Fort Lauderdale News*, Mar. 5, 1988, 65.

[9]Walker, "Houses of Worship"; "West Side Church."

[10]"Local Minister Speaks with President Clinton," *Christian Echo* 84 (Jan. 1994): 10.

[11]"Our Minister," Golden Heights Church of Christ, accessed Sept. 5, 2024, http://www.goldenheightscoc.com/Minister/Index.

[12]Robinson, *Hard-Fighting Soldiers: A History of African American Churches of Christ* (University of Tennessee Press, 2019), 110.

[13]Davis, "Passover Parallels."

[14]Jim Davis, "Rally to Pray for an End to the Atlanta Killings," *Fort Lauderdale News*, Mar. 14, 1981, 99.

[15]Graham, "Black Churches Give More Than Religion," 65; Ken Cummins, "Independent Groups Spending Millions on Bush, Other Races," *South Florida Sun Sentinel*, Nov. 4, 1988, 25.

[16]James D. Davis, Mike Clary, and Marc Freeman, "Obama's Election Sends a Message of Hope, Liberation to Black Churches," *South Florida Sun Sentinel*, Nov. 10, 2008, 3; "Local Minister," 10.

[17]Ardy Friedberg and Valerie Hill-Morgan, "Joy for Jackson," *Fort Lauderdale News*, July 21, 1988, 5; Valerie Hill-Morgan, "Sermons will focus on Mandela," *South Florida Sun Sentinel*, June 24, 1990, 5A; "Local Minister."

[18]Russell Clemings, "Church Offers Reality for Problem Teens," *Fort Lauderdale News*, Apr. 9, 1979, 37.

[19]Interview of W. F. Washington, conducted by Orpheus J. Heyward, April 16, 2024.

[20]Keeble, "News," *Gospel Advocate* 73 (Aug. 20, 1931): 1038; Keeble, "From Brother M. Keeble," *Gospel Advocate* 72 (Aug. 21, 1930): 816; see also "Our History," Woodlawn Forrest Church of Christ, accessed Sept. 5, 2024, https://woodlawnforrest.com/about-us/our-history/.

[21]Robinson, *The Fight Is On in Texas*, 76–77.

[22]"Our Minister," Golden Heights Church of Christ, accessed Sept. 5, 2024, http://www.goldenheightscoc.com/Minister/Index.

The last known photo of Marshall Keeble, taken in April 1968 at Michigan Christian College.

CONCLUSION

AFTER KEEBLE

C. Leonard Allen

Martin Luther King Jr. died on April 4, 1968, in Memphis, Tennessee, from an assassin's bullet. He was thirty-nine years old. Marshall Keeble died on April 20, 1968, in Nashville, Tennessee, at age eighty-nine. Their deaths in the same month stirred controversy in Churches of Christ over race and the Civil Rights Movement, exposing the tensions between those who defended Keeble's silence on race and thus did not question the racial status quo and the growing number of those who argued that things must change.[1]

The Social Aftermath

As we have seen in this book, Keeble, throughout his entire evangelistic career, avoided the subject of segregation. "I don't recall speaking to an audience," he said in an interview near the end of his life, "that I ever said anything about segregation much at all." He did not think Black preachers should address it, because preachers who did "couldn't talk or think of nothing else."[2] Keeble never openly challenged the segregationist status quo; he remained consistently silent. What he did say were things like, "The gospel of Christ will knock out of us all the prejudice and malice we have against any man. It will knock it out. And when it hasn't done so, we haven't absorbed enough of the spirit of Christ."[3]

Floyd Rose, one of Keeble's "preacher boys," once confronted him about his silence on segregation. "Why don't you just tell them? You got to know this [segregation] is wrong. Just tell them! . . . You're the only one they let in their pulpits. You're the only one they let speak in the universities. Tell them!" Keeble listened in silence and then finally responded: "Floyd, you want me to tell them? Then . . . how these kids going to go to school? If I tell them—I hate this as much as you do—but if I tell them, what's going to happen to this school?"[4] There is good evidence to conclude that Keeble disliked the realities of the Jim Crow South as much as anyone. But he believed that, in his time and place, his most effective and important work was preaching the gospel, planting and building up Black churches, and educating their youths. But after his death in April 1968, this quietist view would steadily recede among younger Black leaders in Churches of Christ.

A strong position among White Church of Christ leaders, which came sharply to the forefront following the deaths of Keeble and King in 1968, was that any civil rights activism like King's was out of bounds for Christians. This view had been long in place among Whites by the 1960s. Keeble's death, set alongside King's, provided the platform for showcasing it. In his eulogy of Keeble, for example, Reuel Lemmons declared that Keeble "never led a riot; he never burned out a block of buildings; he never marched on Washington." Astonishingly, he claimed that Keeble "traveled—without discrimination—for seventy years among blacks and whites alike . . . . Indeed, because of his life and work there has been an infinitesimally small amount of racial prejudice in the Church of Christ."[5]

Lemmons's strange claim that Keeble experienced little discrimination drew incredulous responses from Black church leaders. One was the prominent preacher Roosevelt Wells, who wrote to Lemmons: "Your appreciation of black men is limited to those who do not actively and openly protest the shameful unchristian and unAmerican and inhuman treatment the black people of this country have received. . . . In the spirit of Christ, I recommend that you do some research, some soul searching, and some waking up."[6]

The events of 1968 in many ways would mark the end of an era—the era when African American Churches of Christ sought and embraced the patronage of White churches and when the illusion of racial harmony was the normative posture among Whites. The closing of Keeble's Nashville Christian Institute in 1967 and the lawsuit over the disposition of its assets conducted by Fred Gray was an important catalyst—as well as a symbol—of the growing independence of the Black churches. Following 1968, Black church leaders were more and more outspoken in their rejection of White paternalism and in their embrace of a spirit of independence.

An exchange between John Waddey and Roosevelt Wells in 1969 provides a telling example. In an article in the *Christian Echo*, Waddey, a White preacher, attempted to celebrate the easing of racial tensions in the segregated Churches of Christ: "Across the land, white brethren have realized their responsibility to extend the hand of congregational fellowship *to men of any race who want to worship with them.* For this we should thank God." Wells saw here the old spirit of White condescension and paternalism, where Whites adopted the stance that "Father knoweth best." Waddey had joined the throngs of "self-appointed experts who are always advising Black brothers." And Waddey's admonition to "black brethren" not to get involved in "social and political issues" was deeply offensive; although Wells himself had stated publicly that King was not a Christian, he insisted that the spirit of challenging injustices and inequalities, modeled by King, should be embraced by all African American Christians.[7]

After 1968 through the remaining decades of the twentieth century, African American Churches of Christ, as one historian put it, "moved from segregation to independence."[8] Rather than moving closer together in fellowship, the White church and the Black church actually moved further apart. Over the twentieth century, Black churches had developed their own national lectureship, their own journals, their own networks, their own college (Southwestern Christian College). A common view among Black leaders was that the generations of White racism in Churches of Christ had pushed Blacks together to form what eventually became a virtually independent Black Church of Christ.

The Theological Aftermath

Keeble received his theology, as he often acknowledged, from his White mentors who edited the *Gospel Advocate*—David Lipscomb, E. G. Sewell, F. B. Srygley, B. C. Goodpasture, and others; he noted that the magazine had been like a second Bible to him and the Black preachers who influenced him, and he made it a practice over many years to sign up new converts as subscribers. It is not a stretch to say that Keeble's basic theology was shaped primarily by the *Gospel Advocate* and its editors.[9] And it was the source of the theology he passed on to his sons and grandsons in the faith who became the leaders of Black Churches of Christ across the South and beyond.

As we saw in Chapter One, Churches of Christ, in the opening years of the twentieth century, had recently been through a wrenching separation from the Christian Churches and were in the process of rebuilding their movement and clarifying their theology. By 1930 or so, a doctrinal orthodoxy was fairly well in place, although various doctrinal issues would continue to be hashed out. Central to this orthodoxy were two closely related convictions. First, the New Testament church was defined by a clear and strict pattern from which one must not deviate—Alexander Campbell, a hundred years earlier, had called it the "ancient gospel and order of things," and succeeding generations had narrowed and hardened it. And second, any deviation from this pattern disqualified a church from being a true church of Christ. And the reality was that all denominations had deviated from this New Testament pattern and were thereby not true churches. "All denominations are sinful," David Lipscomb had frequently written around the turn of the century. "Every one is formed by adding to the things God ordained."[10] The obvious conclusion was that the Church of Christ was simply "the Lord's church," in contrast to all the denominations.

This conviction—central to Churches of Christ for the first seven decades and more of the twentieth century—was also central to Marshall Keeble's theology throughout his evangelistic career. It formed what Keeble's major biographer called his "radical exclusivism."[11] And it was part of the theological legacy he passed on to his "sons" in the faith.

As we have seen in this book, quite a few younger preachers influenced by Keeble became outspoken critics of—and in some cases activists against—the racism that had been endemic in American culture and among Churches of Christ. One of them, Andrew J. Hairston, took the exclusivist ecclesiology of Keeble and Churches of Christ and turned it back on itself. He charged in 1969 that the sin of racism has "never permitted the true Church to exist in reality on the American frontier; it has only accommodated a denominational Church of Christ that is obviously divided and deeply split asunder by racial antagonisms." Whites had created the segregated system, he added, but Black Christians, to their discredit, "are primarily yet maintaining it."[12] Hairston's take on the doctrine of the true church was unusual, at least in public; after Keeble, the exclusivist theology mostly remained in place among the Black churches.

Thirty years later, by the late 1990s, the exclusivist theology was clearly visible in an episode that grew out of the One in Christ conferences organized by both Black and White leaders. One striking fruit of these gatherings was an apology by the president of Abilene Christian University for its long history of racial discrimination. "We are here today," he said in 1999 before a large assembly of Black church members, "to confess the sins of racism and discrimination and to issue a formal apology to all of you and to ask for your forgiveness."[13] It was a powerful and moving moment.

Plans for a third conference in 2002 began to take shape; it would focus, like the earlier ones, on racial reconciliation. But when the Black organizers began to insist on adding to the agenda a list of doctrinal issues pitting strict conservatives against moderates—*Is the Church of Christ a denomination?*, for example, and *Can one have fellowship with "the denominations"?*—the White organizers withdrew from participation in the conference. They concluded that the focus on racial reconciliation had been derailed and that civil and constructive discussion would be difficult. The Black leaders were dismayed.[14] It seemed that the legacy of "radical exclusivism" had trumped, for the time being at least, the legacy of racial separation.

Reflecting on this episode, Edward Robinson noted a sharp irony in the Keeble legacy:

> The same elitism, antipathy, and arrogance that many whites in the United States exhibited toward black people in the eras of slavery and segregation are now

> espoused by many African Americans in Churches of Christ. [They] denounce their black religious neighbors in other churches, while they rebuke and reject white fellow Christians who accept them. This is the church Marshall Keeble made.[15]

For some decades in White Churches of Christ, a theological shift had been emerging. It was a strong move away from the traditional exclusivist theology (described above) and the emergence of a softer approach to denominationalism, often recognizing as fellow Christians those who confess Christ as Lord and Savior, reflect his character, and seek to follow him in all things. Traditionalists, of course, denounced this tendency all along the way, but this broader perspective continued to grow; not surprisingly, the result has been a de facto split between more traditional White churches and more moderate ones.

Black Churches of Christ had not participated much in these theological tensions. Over these last five decades or so, they tended to maintain the "church that Keeble made"—that is to say, the church formed by the theology of the *Gospel Advocate* in the opening decades of the twentieth century.

Today, nearly sixty years after Keeble's passing, Black Churches of Christ face a new time, new pressures, and a new cultural landscape. The kind of theological tensions and adjustments that have been rising steadily in many White churches for decades are now becoming more visible in the Black churches. Those tensions are taking their own distinctive shape due to the Black churches' distinctive and separate heritage. In the opening chapter, I observed that "all Christian traditions change from one generation to the next. Changes may be subtle, but the very process of passing on a set of beliefs inevitably alters them." That is to say, changing times and the changing of the guard bring theological adjustments and correctives as new leaders assess the fruit of the tradition they have received. We all stand in a tradition. It is a blessing. And inevitably a challenge. We bear the charge to move it forward in a new time.

Our new cultural landscape is clearly post-denominational and indeed post-Christian. Christian faith is much less pervasive and persuasive than it once was, and it no longer provides the primary moral compass and dominant cultural symbols for American culture. Denominational "brands" are coming to matter less and less to more and more people. And there appears to be a fresh and vibrant nondenominational spirit washing over the Christian landscape. Churches of Christ throughout their history, both White and Black, have claimed a nondenominational vision. Now the times are giving them a new chance to live out what they think that means. It will be a challenge—that much we know. And regarding the matter of race, we still find ourselves these many decades later in a crucible. A crucible can be a redemptive place—"a place or situation that forces people to change or make difficult decisions" (*Brittannica Dictionary*).

For fifty-five years, Marshall Keeble was a steadfast, Spirit-gifted, colorful, and inspiring voice whom God used in a remarkable way. We want to honor him, but not only that. We want to better understand what shaped him—his times, his mentors, his theology, and his priorities. And to consider his legacy—and from it to glean wisdom for the uncharted new times that lie ahead.

NOTES

[1]For a recent perspective on Keeble and King, see Hamil R. Harris and Bobby Ross Jr., "Two Legacies, Fifty Years Later," *Christian Chronicle*, Apr. 3, 2018, https://christianchronicle.org/two-legacies-50-years-later/.

[2]J. E. Choate interview with Marshall Keeble (1965–67), cassette recording, Special Collections, Beamon Library, Lipscomb University.

[3]Keeble, "The Church among the Colored," *Abilene Christian College Lectures* (Firm Foundation, 1950), 146.

[4]Interview with Floyd Rose by Barclay Key, June 8, 2005, in Barclay Key, *Race and Restoration: Churches of Christ and the Black Freedom Struggle* (Louisiana State University Press, 2019), 128.

[5]Reuel Lemmons, "Marshall Keeble," *Firm Foundation* (May 14, 1968): 306. Also Gus Nichols, "Dr. Martin Luther King Jr . . . and Some of Our Brethren," *West End Church of Christ Bulletin* (Birmingham, Alabama), Sept. 6, 1968, John Allen Chalk papers, Archives, Harding School of Theology Library, Searcy, Arkansas.

[6]Roosevelt Wells letter quoted by Key, *Race and Restoration*, 139–40.

[7]John Waddey, "A Plea to My Black Brethren," *Christian Echo* 67 (Nov. 1969): 2–3; Roosevelt Wells, "A Reply," *Christian Echo* 67, 2, cited by Crawford, *Shattering the Illusion*, 155.

[8]Crawford, *Shattering the Illusion*. See also David Jones Jr., "Growing Their Separate Ways," *Gospel Advocate* 132 (Jan. 1990): 21–23.

[9]See Robinson, *Show Us How You Do It*, 2nd ed. (2010), 47–55.

[10]David Lipscomb and E. G. Sewell, *Questions Answered* (Gospel Advocate, 1921).

[11]Robinson, *Show Us How You Do It*, 176.

[12]Andrew J. Hairston, "Spiritual Equality in Christ," *Christian Echo* (Oct. 1969): 5.

[13]Royce Money, "Reflections on Apology, Race, and Christian Higher Education," in *Unfinished Reconciliation: Justice, Racism, and Churches of Christ*, eds. Gary Holloway and John York (Abilene Christian University Press, 2013), 173–99.

[14]Money, "Reflections on Apology," 192–95, 198.

[15]Robinson, *Show Us How You Do It*, 176.

APPENDIX ONE

KEEBLE AND CATO

An Unlikely Father and Son

Rita Cato Cochrane

My father, Willie Cato, was privileged to work hand in hand for many years with Marshall Keeble. Theirs was an unorthodox friendship complicated by the time frame of the turbulent sixties when racial segregation plagued not only our nation but our churches. Although our father was a young White minister and Brother Keeble an elderly Black minister, their relationship was so tight that our father lovingly called Keeble "Pop," and Keeble lovingly called Dad "Son."

Escorting Pop to and from his speaking engagements and finding overnight accommodations always presented complications. Cato would drive late into the night, park far from the motel office, most often leave Pop in the car, and go in alone to secure a double room for the night. Then he and Pop would slip into the "whites only" motel room unnoticed. Most of the time this tactic proved successful—but not always.

On one occasion, after stopping for the night at a Texas motel, there was a loud banging on the door at around one o'clock in the morning. Brother Keeble had been spotted as a Black man in a "whites only" motel, and they were being evicted. As my father argued with the young White manager and tempers rose, Brother Keeble remained quiet. He dressed, packed up, and then sat down on the edge of his bed to tie his shoelaces. After a few minutes, Brother Keeble spoke up.

"It's okay, son," he told our father. "We don't stay where we are not wanted. The good Lord brought us this far. The good Lord will take us safely down the road. It's time to go."

Dad and Pop packed the car and departed under the same cover of darkness as they arrived. Heading down the road toward their destination, my father drove in silence. It was Brother Keeble who spoke first.

"Son, you know you have to forgive him, right?" he said.

Of all the graces available to humankind, my father admitted forgiveness was not yet on his radar that night. What my father did admit to were feelings of anger, humiliation, and perhaps a bit of retaliation. But forgiveness had not yet found its way into his heart, for his heart was breaking over the treatment Pop had endured. So Dad responded, "I will, Pop. Just not yet."

It was not until much later that my father, Willie Cato, realized the great lesson Pop taught him about forgiveness on that trip. It was while sitting on his bed and tying his shoes that night that Brother Keeble had forgiven the man who was evicting them. While Dad argued with the manager, Brother Keeble remained quiet so he could pray for the angry motel manager. Extending forgiveness meant Pop was immediately filled with the peace that comes when we forgive, and it allowed him to ride calmly down the road, while Dad was forced to carry a heavy burden of anger and resentment on his shoulders.

Dad recounted this story numerous times through the years, and it always brought a tear to his eyes. But never in his wildest dreams could he see that God was not finished with this story. The final chapter had not yet been written.

Decades following the deaths of both Keeble and Cato, a certain minister from Texas came to Nashville to attend an event at Lipscomb University. Upon learning that one of Willie Cato's children now worked for the university, he sought her out. It seemed this minister volunteered at a nursing home in his Texas town and had met a resident there who had tearfully shared with him a story from his youth. Many years earlier, this man was the night manager for a motel where, due to his racial prejudice and the strong segregationist policy, he had evicted Marshall Keeble and Willie Cato in the middle of the night. For years, the man had anguished over it, longing for forgiveness for his actions. In his last days, knowing that his minister friend was coming to Nashville, the man had prevailed upon the minister to help him settle his final earthly request and seek forgiveness from our father. With our father deceased, my sister, Amy Cato Hamar, was quick to extend grace on Dad's behalf. The minister thanked my sister and left for the nursing home to deliver to this man the peace only forgiveness can offer.

Marshall Keeble (Pop) went to glory in 1968. Willie Cato (Son) followed him in 1991. Keeble's legacy has been recounted in numerous books and articles. One was written by our father, Willie Cato. Its title is *His Hand and Heart*.

APPENDIX TWO

KEEBLE IN HIS OWN WORDS

Two Mentors[1]

While sitting at home on account of such severe weather and studying God's word, I can see so many things to be thankful for. I thank God for that dear old mother that brought me into this great world and instilled that great principle into me to love God and for that father that labored hard to give to his family the necessities of life and took me by the hand and led me to church every Lord's day. We need more parents like these, for a child reared this way will never depart from its training. At the age of fourteen I obeyed the gospel, and I am so thankful that I began to serve the Lord early in life, so I never learned so many evil habits that most young men learn.

When about eighteen years old, I married a daughter of S. W. Womack. I never thought at first what a blessing it was to marry into this Christian man's family, but I am thankful now. If there ever was a Christian anywhere, this old servant is one. While I am young, I am trying to live humble and meek like him, and I thank

God for the impression his life has made on me. Some people send flowers and put them on the casket after death, but I believe in giving them while we live. I am a young preacher endeavoring to make a success in life; and if I can just make the man that Brother Womack is, I will be so thankful. His success in life, in a material way, has not been very great, but I have reference to the great treasure he is laying up in heaven. He has established more churches and done more to keep "digressivism" out of this State than any colored man I know of anywhere; and had it not been for the instruction he received from such men as Brother David Lipscomb and Brother E. G. Sewell, he could not have succeeded as he has. I have been in conversation with him thousands of times on scriptural subjects, and he rarely ever finishes without mentioning one or the other of these great men.

About nineteen years ago Brother A. C. Campbell decided to pull out from "digressivism," and he had courage enough to begin a mission in his own home. As soon as Brother Womack learned of it, he joined hand in hand with him, and they worked for some time in this way, and the interest grew so we had to get a larger place to worship; so we purchased a piece of property on the corner of Jackson Street and Fourteenth Avenue, North, known as the "Jackson Street church of Christ," and we are so thankful for this work that these two worthy Christian preachers have done. Brother Campbell is nearly sixty years of age, but is yet active in the ministry, and I know of no man that is doing more to convert the world than he.

As I have been closely connected with these two brethren for about twenty years or more, I can truthfully say that they have suffered while preaching the gospel, and their wives need to be praised for their great endurance, and for all of this we thank the Lord. It was these two men that encouraged me to preach the gospel and I shall never be through praising them and thanking God for such blessings. Neither of these men know that I am writing this article. I just thought it proper to say a few words about the good they are doing and have done. Brother Womack and Brother Campbell say that the *Gospel Advocate* has been second with them, and the Bible first.

Speaking concerning the *Advocate*, it has been a great help to me in studying the Bible. I have been reading it ever since I learned to read. My grandfather took it until his death; then, after I married into Brother Womack's family, I found it there. So I am still reading it. May God bless and lead those in whose hands the paper is to remain, and may it go forth blessing the world as it did when that great and noble servant, David Lipscomb, lived. Some brethren think that the paper will not be what it used to be, but I believe such men as J. C. McQuiddy, A. B. Lipscomb, and T. B. Larimore are fully able in every sense to cause the paper to hold its present position in the world, and, like Joshua, they will lead us across the Jordan. For all of these rich blessings we thank our Heavenly Father.

Death of S. W. Womack (1920)[2]

On July 13, 1920, Brother S. W. Womack departed this life. He had been sick for nearly two years, and had been confined to his room about ten months. His suffering was great at times, but he never once murmured, but was cheerful all the time. I was absent when he died. I was in a meeting at Latham, Tenn., and they wired me three or four messages, but I failed to get either one until it was too late for me to attend the funeral. It had been my desire to be present at this good man's funeral. Old Brother Clay, who had labored with him for years, spoke over the remains; also Brother Dowell, a young brother who is a product of Jackson Street church, spoke encouraging words. Brother F. W. Smith and Brother A. B. Lipscomb were present and spoke words of comfort, and all who heard them were uplifted and edified. Brother A. M. Burton was also present. This Christian man never talks much in a public way, but his life tells what he is. These brethren were all interested in Brother Womack and his work, and during his life of over forty years in the ministry they greatly helped in supporting him in his work.

I have often heard Brother Womack say he had gone to places to preach where there was not a colored member of the church of Christ, and his own race would fail to aid or support him, and the white people would supply his needs; and I believe if there ever was a dollar safely invested, it was when given to this faithful preacher of the gospel.

I married in this family about twenty-five years ago, and I have been closely connected with him ever since, and I must say that I never heard him speak rashly or get angry. He seemed to keep a joyful spirit all the time. He has been a great help to me. He first got me to see that I was wrong while working with the "digressives," and I came out from them over twenty years ago, and from that time on I tried to make my life like his; and though he is gone, I shall continue to try and imitate the Christian life he has left behind.

Last September he was with me at Sugar Grove, Ky., where I was holding a meeting. He established this congregation and was highly esteemed by them all. While there he was very feeble and told them that he would never meet them on earth any more, but to live so they could meet on the other side of Jordan.

His funeral was conducted at the Jackson Street church, where he worshiped when at home, and when he got so weak he had to walk with a stick, he would often preach to the congregation while sitting in a chair. He considered this congregation to be the cream of his labors; and although some time ago some trouble arose and caused division, he remained and endeavored to unite us again and stop the division, and we who remain are yet working and praying that unity may be brought about in the future. The Jackson Street Church never once neglected him in any way. They contributed regularly to him, and the members were always giving him something to comfort him in his sickness. Other churches would send donations to him often. The white brethren and sisters all over the South sent him comforting messages. Some of them would say they had never seen him, but they had read of his life in the *Gospel Advocate*.

It was Brother Womack's delight when he was in town to visit the *Gospel Advocate* office, because, he said, he was always made welcome by the whole staff. Whenever he got puzzled over any passage of scripture, he would always have a conference with old Brother David Lipscomb during his life time. After Brother Lipscomb died, he continued to go and talk with Brethren A. B. Lipscomb, J. C. McQuiddy, F. W. Smith, and others, and by this means he was always prepared to instruct his people. He always read his Bible daily.

Brother Womack leaves a faithful wife, two daughters, two grandchildren, and a host of relatives and friends to mourn his departure. "Be thou faithful unto death, and I will give thee a crown of life" (Rev. 2:10 [KJ21]).

Gospel Meetings (1935)[3]

Nashville, Tennessee—Eighty-six baptisms, including five "denominational preachers"

Port Arthur, Texas—Forty-six baptisms, including several "denominational preachers"

Nashville, Tennessee (sponsored by Belmont Church of Christ)—Thirty-four baptisms, with several "denominational preachers"

Chattanooga, Tennessee (sponsored by all the white congregations in the area)—Seventy-five baptized. Keeble says he preached in the largest tent he had seen, seating 1,500, but it would not accommodate all the people.

Fort Worth, Texas (sponsored by the white churches)—no number of baptisms given

Tyler, Texas (sponsored by white churches)—Forty-five baptisms, including several preachers and a lawyer

Abilene, Texas (sponsored by white churches)—Fourteen baptisms. Meeting held in a warehouse seating two thousand people.

Houston, Texas (Heights Church of Christ)—Thirty-two baptisms (two big tents put together)

Little Rock, Arkansas (sponsored by white churches)—Six baptisms

Conway, Arkansas (sponsored by white churches)—Ninety-two baptisms. Attendance about two thousand each night

The Church among the Colored (1950)[4]

Somebody said the southern problem and the northern problem. When you meet my brethren in Christ in the north, in the south, in the east, in the west, there is no problem. My brethren in Christ today, white, are looking out every way possible to bring the negro to Christ, north, south, east, and west. I see no problem. Only thing I see is this: let's carry the gospel to the lost souls of the world. And if the young man needs preparing to carry it, let's establish an institution where he can get the preparation, where he can be prepared, where he can be able to meet these intellectual giants that come out of these sectarian colleges. I don't have nothing to boast about, but I'm just bragging a little.

Now then, somebody is worried about whether a mixed faculty will work. That has come up and naturally it would come up; some white people on the faculty and some colored—will that work? Gentlemen, if it'll work in a sectarian school, it ought to work better in a school where everybody is a Christian. Fisk University, a congregational school, had a white president and white people on the faculty for the last seventy-five years and we have more of the spirit of Christ than they had, I think. Don't get excited—it's God working trying to lift the people that have been possibly misled. And now your hearts are running out for them. The very spirit of Christ is in your heart or you wouldn't be interested in us.

It's the interest of the church of Christ that has missionaries in Africa, it's the interest of the church of Christ in America that sent Brother McMillan and the missionaries to Japan after they had stabbed us in the back. That's fine. That's the spirit of Christ. I believe these missionaries have forgot that attack at Pearl Harbor. The gospel of Christ will knock out of us all the prejudice and malice we have against any man. It will knock it out. And when it hasn't done so, we haven't absorbed enough of the spirit of Christ. Gentlemen, I must appeal to you. This has been my experience for the last fifty years, working with both races, and the colored people are anxious to be led. . . .

I am in sympathy for the gospel preacher in the church of Christ. Why? He stands up to preach in frigidaire. The congregation sits out there and try to free[ze] him. Some good pious brother just looks like a cake of ice looking at him. When I find one trying to freeze me I don't look at him no more. I want to say a word to the young gospel preacher. Don't get discouraged when they try to freeze you, 'cause they know a little more than you do and you're just making your first effort of all and they'll try to freeze you. But don't get excited—you'll make it. I want to tell you what to do. When you see one trying to freeze you, you do like you do with your modern Frigidaire—turn on your defroster. That's right. That's right. I've got a defroster on you all this evening; that's the reason you're smiling and encouraging me. You started in here freezing, but I have you defrosted.

I hope and pray that the day will come when we all can see this school [Southwestern Christian College] . . . [as] one of the greatest colleges in the world, educating boys and girls of the Negro race and preparing them to get out and meet anybody that rises up against the church of Christ. And these men [the White administrators] will rejoice and when they are in their graves, beneath the sod, they will live in the hearts of these young men that go out and preach the gospel to a lost and dying world . . . .

I now conclude with this thought. May the grace of God dwell in your heart and may the grace of God cause you to look upon no race as being inferior, but let's make him what he ought to be and lift him on a higher plane that Jesus can bless you and give you a crown that fadeth not away.

False Doctrine (1952)[5]

There is so much false teaching until it is hard to tell what is true. Men have added so much to God's word unless you read the word of God you will be misled. We are told not to add to God's word (Rev. 22:18, 19). And those who are guilty of adding or subtracting from God's word must reap what they sow. By studying the Scriptures we can keep false teachers from misleading us.

When we are taught to "get religion" we are taught a false doctrine and this is also adding to God's word. When we are taught sprinkling is baptism, we are taught false doctrine. The word of God teaches that baptism is a burial and if we believe that sprinkling is baptism we are letting people mislead us. I would advise anyone not to believe it, because they that teach such are adding to God's word. The Bible teaches that we are buried with Christ by baptism unto death (Rom. 6:4), not sprinkled into Christ. We are also taught by some false teachers that our sins are forgiven before baptism. If this is true why does the word of God teach us that are sins are washed away in baptism? (Acts 22:16). We are also taught that any church will do. But again the Bible teaches that Christ purchased only one church with his blood (Acts 20:28). Such false teaching has confused the world. Jesus taught that he would build his church (Matt. 16:18). He built only one and he gave the apostles the keys to the kingdom, the church. So in order to not be misled by false teachers we must follow the apostles, not the doctrines of men. It is a dangerous thing to be misled. Jesus taught that false teaching is vain (Matt. 15:8, 14). Let me beg all who have been misled by false teachers to search the Scriptures (John 5:39).

Sound Doctrine (1956)[6]

Paul said to Titus, "Speak thou things which befit the sound doctrine" (Titus 2:1). This means that our preaching and conversation must become sound doctrine. When we allow ourselves to destroy the influence and character of our fellow man, we are doing something that does not become sound doctrine. Many of us take delight in slaughtering our brother in Christ. This ought not to be.

A good many times, we go to places to preach, and we start off trying to see if the church is sound in the doctrine, and to see if the regular preacher is sound or comes up to our standard. I am often asked if I believe in certain things. When they ask these questions, they are trying to see if I am sound in the doctrine. I always tell them I believe the apostles' doctrine, and I stand on it. Some of my best friends have told me when I became connected with the Nashville Christian Institute, I ceased to be a sound gospel preacher. But when I began to travel with my little boys, the brethren, who once said, this school connection made me unsound, now say I am sound in doctrine. When they hear these boys preaching, they know that I am doing the right thing in training them. But they misunderstood what I was doing. After a demonstration with the boys they were convinced.

A few years ago, when I held a meeting in one of our cities, one of the brethren told the regular preacher at that place that if he allowed me to take a collection during the meeting, he would never help him in that work again. But I asked for the congregation one afternoon to give a contribution to the school and when the offering was counted, they found a check for one hundred dollars from the man that didn't want the collection taken. After hearing the boys preach that afternoon many of the brethren were convinced that I am a sound gospel preacher.

We must always speak the things that befit sound doctrine. When Peter refused to preach the gospel to the Gentiles, he had to be converted. After God converted him on the house top, he became a sound gospel preacher (Acts 10:1, 34). He converted the first Gentiles to become Christian. But he became unsound again in Antioch and Paul had to rebuke him to his face. Peter today is a good pattern for a sound gospel preacher to follow.

We are also taught to use sound speech that cannot be condemned. And to follow a pattern of good works we must also be sound enough in doctrine and in practice to teach men to follow us. We should not bite and devour one another (Gal. 5:15). The church gradually commits suicide by hating one another. We must be so sound in doctrine, that when we are persecuted for righteousness, we will rejoice and be exceedingly glad (Matt. 5:11, 12). We should prove all things and hold fast to that which is good

(1 Thess. 5:21). We will then take the word of Christ. Brethren, let us have love that hides a multitude of sins, and that will make us love our enemies. When Peter denied his Lord, Jesus had enough love in his heart to forgive him, and allow Peter to preach the first sermon on Pentecost. We would have told Peter that we meant to let him preach that first sermon, but after he sinned, we changed our mind. But Jesus let him preach it. Thank God.

Closing of Nashville Christian Institute (1967)[7]

It's been a long time since I started training boys and girls at Nashville Christian Institute. Since that time, Sister Keeble and I have loved, worked, and given our lives to see this work done. We plan to continue to help young people.

If we continue to help young people here at Nashville Christian Institute, we face many problems. The problems are increasing. Accreditation, this is a must. Everywhere I go, my people ask about this. Used to be, we didn't know about this; so we didn't ask.

We need more ground. The State tells you that you have to have so many acres. We don't have acres; we have a few city lots that we have recently bought. We must have a new building. Everybody wants to live in a new house now, so we've got to have one here at the school. We have bought some new equipment, but we sure need more.

Our teachers are important in our work. Our teachers have never been paid like most other teachers, but they have kept teaching. Some would leave for more money. Right now our teachers' salaries are less than half of the amount paid public school teachers. That tells you why they would leave.

Our enrollment is getting smaller each year. My people are now flocking to the finer schools, which are now open to all races. These schools are closer to them, so they don't have to ride the bus. They can go free; you know we like things that don't cost nothing.

If we continue to operate as a school, we must spend several million dollars. This would include a new location. This would have to be big enough for a new elementary and a new high school building. Even if we did this, we don't know whether the public would appreciate it enough to give to help us, or send us their children. They may say, "Well we've got the same thing right across the street."

Brother A. M. Burton was always interested in my race of people, he loved everybody, but he always helped me and my people. While Brother Burton was still living, he appointed some men from the Board and the President of our school to study our needs, our problems, and how we could best serve the Negro boy and girl. After spending months, looking at our work and examining all the facts as well as seeing the many needs that we have, the committee recommended to the Board that the Nashville Christian Institute close its doors at the end of the school term. That will be June 2, 1967. They also recommended that everything the school owns should be sold and the cash be put into the A. M. Burton–Marshall Keeble Scholarship Fund of the David Lipscomb College Foundation. That's a fund that Brother Burton started before he died. He wanted to help Negro boys and girls get a college education. Praise God for such a man.

While Sister Keeble and I regret to see Nashville Christian Institute close her doors, we wholly support what we thought had to be done. We live in a new day. We must be part of that new day, there is no other way.

I shall continue to work in behalf of Christian education everywhere. Especially, I want to work for the A. M. Burton–Marshall Keeble Scholarship Fund. You know, I'd want to do that because that's got my name.

Since the action has been taken by the Board, Jackson Street church of Christ here in Nashville has given $1,000 to the A. M.

Burton–Marshall Keeble Scholarship Fund. That's the congregation where I have been a member all my life. The Liberty City church of Christ in Miami, Florida has given $550 to this fund. I'm asking all of you who are concerned about my race of people to help the most promising of these young people get a Christian education at David Lipscomb College. These talented young people need to be prepared to serve God.

No one could regret the closing of our school more than Sister Keeble and I, but we must change. Times have changed, so please accept this change. Please throw your help behind it. Please give to the A. M. Burton–Marshall Keeble Scholarship Fund. Please help us fund deserving Negro boys and girls to educate.

NOTES

[1]The following text is from Keeble, "Things That We Should Be Thankful For," *Gospel Advocate* 60, no. 7 (Feb. 14, 1918): 162–63.

[2]The following text is from Keeble, "A Great Man Gone," *Gospel Advocate* 62, no. 31 (July 29, 1920): 744–45.

[3]All data for 1935 meetings found in Marshall Keeble, letter to B. C. Goodpasture, January 1, 1936, B. C. Goodpasture Papers, Box 4, Special Collections, Abilene Christian University Library.

[4]The following text is from Keeble, "The Church among the Colored," a lecture presented at Abilene Christian College, Feb. 23, 1950, *Abilene Christian College Lectures* (Firm Foundation, 1950), 142–56 [excerpts].

[5]The following text is from Keeble, "Among the Colored Brethren," *Gospel Advocate* 94 (Mar. 13, 1952): 174–75.

[6]The following text is from Keeble, "Among the Colored Brethren" *Gospel Advocate* 98 (Oct. 18, 1956): 855.

[7]The following text is from Keeble, "Nashville Christian Institute to Close," *Gospel Advocate* 109 (Mar. 16, 1967): 166.

CONTRIBUTORS

C. Leonard Allen serves as dean of the College of Bible and Ministry at Lipscomb University in Nashville. He taught theology, ethics, and philosophy for many years at Abilene Christian University, Biola University, Fuller Theological Seminary, and John Brown University. He has spoken widely on college campuses and in churches over the past thirty-five years on biblical, historical, and theological themes. He is the author of numerous books, including, *The Cruciform Church: Becoming a Cross-Shaped People in a Secular World, Distant Voices: Discovering a Forgotten Past for a Changing Church, Things Unseen: Churches of Christ in (and after) the Modern Age, Poured Out: The Spirit of God Empowering the Mission of God*, and most recently, *The Bookroom: Remembrance and Forgiveness—A Memoir.*

Tanya Smith Brice serves as provost and vice president of academic affairs at Saint Martin's University, Lacey, Washington. Previously, she served as vice president of education at the Council on Social Work Education in Alexandria, Virginia. She has served on the faculties of the University of South Carolina, Abilene Christian University, and Baylor University. She was recognized as the 2021 Distinguished Alumni of the Year, School of Social Work, University of North Carolina at Chapel Hill. She provides consultation to community organizations, religious institutions, and educational institutions on the impact of their policies on African American families. She was the editor of *Reconciliation Reconsidered: Advancing the National Conversation on Race in Churches of Christ* (2016).

Jefferson R. Caruthers Jr. has served as preaching minister of the Carver Road Church of Christ in Winston-Salem, North Carolina, since 2005. Prior to that he ministered to the Central Avenue Church of Christ, Coldwater, Mississippi (1983–93), and to the Adams Avenue Church of Christ, Cleveland, Ohio (1994–2005). Since 2014 he has served as an instructor in the School of Religious Studies, Little Rock, Arkansas. He serves as Board Chair of Quality Education Schools (a charter school), Winston-Salem, North Carolina, and on the Board of Directors of the National Teachers Workshop of Churches of Christ (2008 to present). His father, J. R. Caruthers Sr., attended the Nashville Christian Institute (1948–51) under the leadership of Marshall Keeble.

Rita Cato Cochrane was born and raised in Nashville, Tennessee, and received her degree in education from Lipscomb University. Her father, Willie Cato, was a minister of the gospel who worked closely with Marshall Keeble for many years. Rita is married to Michael Cochrane, and they are parents of three adult children and grandparents to six rambunctious boys. She taught middle school for twenty-five years and currently serves as the director of women's ministries at the Church of Christ in Green Hills, Nashville. She speaks and teaches for conferences, lectureships, and ladies' days in the United States and abroad. She is the author of two books, *Lace Up Those Sneakers, Let's Take a Walk with God* and *Untying Yesterday's Knots*. She serves on the board of Healing Hands International.

Orpheus J. Heyward serves as senior minister of the Renaissance Church of Christ, Atlanta, Georgia. Under his ministry, Renaissance, originally known as the West End Church of Christ, has become one of the largest African American Churches of Christ in the nation. Heyward has been involved with pastoral work for twenty years and continues to guide churches across the country with church growth and development strategies. He serves as a faculty affiliate in the College of Bible & Ministry at Lipscomb University, Nashville, Tennessee. He is the founder of the Nehemiah Summit, an annual leadership conference in Atlanta that serves church ministry teams. He is author of *God's Word: The Inspiration and Authority of Scripture* (2021) and other writings.

John Mark Hicks has taught systematic and historical theology for thirty-eight years in institutions of higher learning among Churches of Christ. He has taught at Alabama Christian School of Religion (now Amridge University), Magnolia Bible College, Harding School of Theology, and Hazelip School of Theology, Lipscomb University, Nashville. He has authored and edited many books, including *Kingdom Come: Embracing the Legacy of David Lipscomb and James Harding* (with Bobby Valentine), *Come to the Table: Revisioning the Lord's Supper*, *Resisting Babel: Allegiance to God and the Problem of Government* (editor), *Meeting God at* The Shack*: A Journey into Spiritual Recovery*, *Searching for the Pattern: My Journey in Interpreting the Bible*, and *Around the Bible in 80 Days: The Story of God from Creation to New Creation*.

David G. Holmes serves as dean of the College of Liberal Arts and Sciences at Lipscomb University, Nashville. Prior to that, he was professor of English at Pepperdine University for twenty-three years, during which time he served as director of American Studies and later director of African American Studies. He is the author of *Revisiting Racialized Voices: African American Ethos in Language and Literature* (Southern Illinois University Press,

2004) and *Where the Sacred and Secular Harmonize: Birmingham Mass Meeting Rhetoric and the Prophetic Legacy of the Civil Rights Movement* (Cascade, 2017), as well as numerous book chapters and essays. He has delivered guest lectures at a number of colleges and universities around the country.

Edward J. Robinson has taught history and Bible at Abilene Christian University, Southwestern Christian College, and Texas College. His biography of Marshall Keeble, *Show Us How You Do It: Marshall Keeble and the Rise of Black Churches of Christ, 1914–1968*, was published in 2008 and stands as the major scholarly work on Keeble. His other books include *Hard-Fighting Soldiers: A History of African American Churches of Christ* (2019), *I Was Under a Heavy Burden: The Life of Annie C. Tuggle, A Godsend to His People: The Essential Writings and Speeches of Marshall Keeble* (2008), and *The Fight Is On in Texas: A History of African American Churches of Christ in the Lone Star State, 1865–2000* (2008). His most recent book is *To Pave the Way for His People: A Life of Preston Taylor* (2023).